THE R[...]
THE SOLDIER

by

REBECCA WEST

COMPASS CIRCLE

The Return of the Soldier.
Current edition published by Compass Circle in 2019.

Published by Compass Circle
Cover copyright ©2019 by Compass Circle.

All rights reserved. No part of this publication may be reproduced, stored in a retrieval system, or transmitted, in any form or by any means, electronic, mechanical, photocopying, recording or otherwise without the prior permission of the publisher.

Note:
All efforts have been made to preserve original spellings and punctuation of the original edition which may include old-fashioned English spellings of words and archaic variants.

This book is a product of its time and does not reflect the same views on race, gender, sexuality, ethnicity, and interpersonal relations as it would if it were written today.

For information contact :
information@compass-circle.com

It's the soul's duty to be loyal to its own desires. It must abandon itself to its master passion.

REBECCA WEST

SECRET WISDOM OF THE AGES SERIES

Life presents itself, it advances in a fast way. Life indeed never stops. It never stops until the end. The most diverse questions peek and fade in our minds. Sometimes we seek for answers. Sometimes we just let time go by.

The book you have now in your hands has been waiting to be discovered by you. This book may reveal the answers to some of your questions.

Books are friends. Friends who are always by your side and who can give you great ideas, advice or just comfort your soul.

A great book can make you see things in your soul that you have not yet discovered, make you see things in your soul that you were not aware of.

Great books can change your life for the better. They can make you understand fascinating theories, give you new ideas, inspire you to undertake new challenges or to walk along new paths.

Literature Classics like the one of *The Return of the Soldier* are indeed a secret to many, but for those of us lucky enough to have discovered them, by one way or another, these books can enlighten us. They can open a wide range of possibilities to us. Because achieving greatness requires knowledge.

The series SECRET WISDOM OF THE AGES presented by Compass Circle try to bring you the great timeless masterpieces of literature, autobiographies and personal development,.

We welcome you to discover with us fascinating works by Nathaniel Hawthorne, Sir Arthur Conan Doyle, Edith Wharton, among others.

CHAPTER 1

"**A**H, don't begin to fuss!" wailed Kitty. "If a woman began to worry in these days because her husband hadn't written to her for a fortnight! Besides, if he'd been anywhere interesting, anywhere where the fighting was really hot, he'd have found some way of telling me instead of just leaving it as 'Somewhere in France.' He'll be all right."

We were sitting in the nursery. I had not meant to enter it again, now that the child was dead; but I had come suddenly on Kitty as she slipped the key into the lock, and I had lingered to look in at the high room, so full of whiteness and clear colors, so unendurably gay and familiar, which is kept in all respects as though there were still a child in the house. It was the first lavish day of spring, and the sunlight was pouring through the tall, arched windows and the flowered curtains so brightly that in the old days a fat fist would certainly have been raised to point out the new, translucent glories of the rosebud. Sunlight was lying in great pools on the blue cork floor and the soft rugs, patterned with strange beasts, and threw dancing beams, which should have been gravely watched for hours, on the white paint and the blue distempered walls. It fell on the rocking-horse, which had been Chris's idea of an appropriate present for his year-old son, and showed what a fine fellow he was and how tremendously dappled; it picked out Mary and her little lamb on the chintz ottoman.

And along the mantelpiece, under the loved print of the snarling tiger, in attitudes that were at once angular and relaxed, as though they were ready for play at their master's pleasure, but found it hard to keep from drowsing in this warm weather, sat the Teddy Bear and the chimpanzee and the woolly white dog and the black cat with eyes that roll. Everything was there except Oliver. I turned away so that I might not spy on Kitty revisiting her dead. But she called after me:

"Come here, Jenny. I'm going to dry my hair." And when I looked again I saw that her golden hair was all about her shoulders and that she wore over her frock a little silken jacket trimmed with rosebuds. She looked so like a girl on a magazine cover that one expected to find a large "15 cents" somewhere attached to her person. She had taken Nanny's big basket-chair from its place by the high-chair, and was pushing it over to the middle window. "I always come in here when Emery has washed my hair. It's the sunniest room in the house. I wish Chris wouldn't have it kept as a nursery when there's no chance—" She sat down, swept her hair over the back of the chair into the sunlight, and held out to me her tortoiseshell hair-brush. "Give it a brush now and then, like a good soul; but be careful. Tortoise snaps so!"

I took the brush and turned to the window, leaning my forehead against the glass and staring unobservantly at the view. You probably know the beauty of that view; for when Chris rebuilt Baldry Court after his marriage he handed it over to architects who had not so much the wild eye of the artist as the knowing wink of the manicurist, and between them they massaged the dear old place into matter for innumerable photographs in the illustrated papers. The house lies on the crest of Harrowweald, and from its windows the eye drops to miles of emerald pasture-land lying wet and brilliant under a westward line of sleek hills; blue with distance and distant woods, while nearer it range the suave decorum of the lawn and the Lebanon cedar, the branches of which are like darkness made palpable, and the minatory gauntnesses of the topmost pines in the wood that breaks downward, its bare boughs a close texture of browns and purples, from the pond on the edge of the hill.

That day its beauty was an affront to me, because, like most Englishwomen of my time, I was wishing for the return of a soldier. Disregarding the national interest and everything else except the keen prehensile gesture of our hearts toward him, I wanted to snatch my Cousin Christopher from the wars and seal him in this green pleasantness his wife and I now looked upon. Of late I had had bad dreams about him. By nights I saw Chris running across the brown rottenness of No-Man's-Land, starting back here because he trod upon a hand, not even looking there because of the awfulness of an unburied head, and not till my dream was packed full of horror did I see him pitch forward on his knees as he reached safety, if it was that. For on the war-films I have seen men slip down as softly from the trench-parapet, and none but the grimmer philosophers could say that they had reached safety by their fall. And when I escaped into wakefulness it was only to lie stiff and think of stories I had heard in the boyish voice of the modern subaltern, which rings indomitable, yet has most of its gay notes flattened: "We were all of us in a barn one night, and a shell came along. My pal sang out, 'Help me, old man; I've got no legs!' and I had to answer, 'I can't, old man; I've got no hands!'" Well, such are the dreams of Englishwomen to-day. I could not complain, but I wished for the return of our soldier. So I said:

"I wish we could hear from Chris. It is a fortnight since he wrote."

And then it was that Kitty wailed, "Ah, don't begin to fuss!" and bent over her image in a hand-mirror as one might bend for refreshment over scented flowers.

I tried to build about me such a little globe of ease as always ensphered her, and thought of all that remained good in our lives though Chris was gone. I was sure that we were preserved from the reproach of luxury, because we had made a fine place for Chris, one little part of the world that was, so far as surfaces could make it so, good enough for his amazing goodness. Here we had nourished that surpassing amiability which was so habitual that one took it as one of his physical characteristics, and regarded any lapse into bad temper as a calamity as startling as the breaking of a leg; here we had made happiness inevitable for him. I could shut my eyes and think of innumerable proofs of how well we had succeeded, for there never was so visibly contented a man. And I recalled all that he did one morning just a year ago when he went to the front.

First he had sat in the morning-room and talked and stared out on the lawns that already had the desolation of an empty stage, although he had not yet gone; then broke off suddenly and went about the house, looking into many rooms. He went to the stables and looked at the horses and had the dogs brought out; he refrained from touching them or speaking to them, as though he felt himself already infected with the squalor of war and did not want to contaminate their bright physical well-being. Then he went to the edge of the wood and stood staring down into the clumps of dark-leaved rhododendrons and the yellow tangle of last year's bracken and the cold winter black of the trees. (From this very window I had spied on him.) Then he moved broodingly back to the house to be with his wife until the moment of his going, when Kitty and I stood on the steps to see him motor off to Waterloo. He kissed us both. As he bent over me I noticed once again how his hair was of two colors, brown and gold. Then he got into the car, put on his Tommy air, and said: "So long! I'll write you from Berlin!" and as he spoke his head dropped back, and he set a hard stare on the house. That meant, I knew, that he loved the life he had lived with us and desired to carry with him to the dreary place of death and dirt the complete memory of everything about his home, on which his mind could brush when things were at their worst, as a man might finger an amulet through his shirt. This house, this life with us, was the core of his heart.

"If he could come back!" I said. "He was so happy here!"

And Kitty answered:

"He could not have been happier."

It was important that he should have been happy, for, you see, he was not like other city men. When we had played together as children in that wood he had always shown great faith in the imminence of the improbable. He thought that the birch-tree would really stir and shrink and quicken into an enchanted princess, that he really was a red Indian, and that his disguise would suddenly fall from him at the right sundown, that at any moment a tiger might lift red fangs through the bracken, and he expected these things with a stronger motion of the imagination than the ordinary child's make-believe. And from a thousand intimations, from his occasional clear fixity of gaze on good things as though they were about to dissolve into better, from the passionate anticipation with which he went to new countries or met new people, I was aware that this faith had persisted into his adult life. He had exchanged his expectation of becoming a red Indian for the equally wistful aspiration of becoming completely reconciled to life. It was his hopeless hope that some time he would have an experience that would act on his life like alchemy, turning to gold all the dark metals of events, and from that revelation he would go on his way rich with an inextinguishable joy. There had been, of course, no chance of his ever getting it. Literally there wasn't room to swing a revelation in his crowded life. First of all, at his father's death he had been obliged to take over a business that was weighted by the needs of a mob of female relatives who were all useless either in the old way, with antimacassars, or in the new way, with golf-clubs; then Kitty had come along and picked up his conception of normal expenditure, and carelessly stretched it as a woman stretches a new glove on her hand. Then there had been the difficult task of learning to live after the death of his little son. It had lain on us, the responsibility, which gave us dignity, to compensate him for his lack of free adventure by arranging him a gracious life. But now, just because our performance had been so brilliantly adequate, how dreary was the empty stage!

We were not, perhaps, specially contemptible women, because nothing could ever really become a part of our life until it had been referred to Chris's attention. I remember thinking, as the parlor-maid came in with a card on the tray, how little it mattered who had called and what flag of prettiness or wit she flew, since there was no chance that Chris would come in and stand over her, his fairness red in the firelight, and show her that detached attention, such as an unmusical man pays to good music, which men of anchored affections give to attractive women.

Kitty read from the card:

"'Mrs. William Grey, Mariposa, Ladysmith Road, Weald-stone,' I don't know anybody in *Wealdstone*." That is the name of the red suburban stain which fouls the fields three miles nearer London than Harrowweald. One cannot now protect one's environment as one once could. "Do I know her, Ward? Has she been here before?"

"Oh, no, ma'am." The parlor-maid smiled superciliously. "She said she had news for you." From her tone one could deduce an over-confiding explanation made by a shabby visitor while using the door-mat almost too zealously.

Kitty pondered, then said:

"I'll come down." As the girl went, Kitty took up the amber hair-pins from her lap and began swathing her hair about her head. "Last year's fashion," she commented; "but I fancy it'll do for a person with that sort of address." She stood up, and threw her little silk dressing-jacket over the rocking-horse. "I'm seeing her because she may need something, and I specially want to be kind to people while Chris is away. One wants to deserve well of heaven." For a minute she was aloof in radiance, but as we linked arms and went out into the corridor she became more mortal, with a pout. "The people that come breaking into one's nice, quiet day!" she moaned reproachfully, and as we came to the head of the broad stair-case she leaned over the white balustrade to peer down on the hall, and squeezed my arm. "Look!" she whispered.

Just beneath us, in one of Kitty's prettiest chintz arm-chairs, sat a middle-aged woman. She wore a yellowish raincoat and a black hat with plumes. The sticky straw hat had only lately been renovated by something out of a little bottle bought at the chemist's. She had rolled her black thread gloves into a ball on her lap, so that she could turn her gray alpaca skirt well above her muddy boots and adjust its brush-braid with a seamed red hand that looked even more worn when she presently raised it to touch the glistening flowers of the pink azalea that stood on a table beside her. Kitty shivered, then muttered:

"Let's get this over," and ran down the stairs. On the last step she paused and said with conscientious sweetness, "Mrs. Grey!"

"Yes," answered the visitor. She lifted to Kitty a sallow and relaxed face the expression of which gave me a sharp, pitying pang of prepossession in her favor: it was beautiful that so plain a woman should so ardently rejoice in another's loveliness. "Are you Mrs. Baldry?" she asked, almost as if she were glad about it, and stood up. The bones of her bad stays clicked as she moved. Well, she was not so bad. Her body was long and round and shapely, and with a noble squareness of the shoulders; her fair hair curled diffidently about a good brow; her gray eyes, though they were remote, as if anything worth looking at in her life had kept a long way off, were full of tenderness; and though she was slender, there was something about her of the wholesome, endearing heaviness of the ox or the trusted big dog. Yet she was bad enough. She was repulsively furred with neglect and poverty, as even a good glove that has dropped down behind a bed in a hotel and has lain undisturbed for a day or two is repulsive when the chambermaid retrieves it from the dust and fluff.

She flung at us as we sat down:

"My general maid is sister to your second housemaid."

It left us at a loss.

"You've come about a reference?" asked Kitty.

"Oh, no. I've had Gladys two years now, and I've always found her a very good girl. I want no reference." With her finger-nail she followed the burst seam of the dark pigskin

8

purse that slid about on her shiny alpaca lap. "But girls talk, you know. You mustn't blame them." She seemed to be caught in a thicket of embarrassment, and sat staring up at the azalea.

With the hardness of a woman who sees before her the curse of women's lives, a domestic row, Kitty said that she took no interest in servants' gossip.

"Oh, it isn't—" her eyes brimmed as though we had been unkind—"servants' gossip that I wanted to talk about. I only mentioned Gladys"—she continued to trace the burst seam of her purse—"because that's how I heard you didn't know."

"What don't I know?"

Her head drooped a little.

"About Mr. Baldry. Forgive me, I don't know his rank."

"Captain Baldry," supplied Kitty, wonderingly. "What is it that I don't know?"

She looked far away from us, to the open door and its view of dark pines and pale March sunshine, and appeared to swallow something.

"Why, that he's hurt," she gently said.

"Wounded, you mean?" asked Kitty.

Her rusty plumes oscillated as she moved her mild face about with an air of perplexity.

"Yes," she said, "he's wounded."

Kitty's bright eyes met mine, and we obeyed that mysterious human impulse to smile triumphantly at the spectacle of a fellow-creature occupied in baseness. For this news was not true. It could not possibly be true. The War Office would have wired to us immediately if Chris had been wounded. This was such a fraud as one sees recorded in the papers that meticulously record squalor in paragraphs headed, "Heartless Fraud on Soldier's Wife." Presently she would say that she had gone to some expense to come here with her news and that she was poor, and at the first generous look on our faces there would come some tale of trouble that would disgust the imagination by pictures of yellow-wood furniture that a landlord oddly desired to seize and a pallid child with bandages round its throat. I cast down my eyes and shivered at the horror. Yet there was something about the physical quality of the woman, unlovely though she was, which preserved the occasion from utter baseness. I felt sure that had it not been for the tyrannous emptiness of that evil, shiny pigskin purse that jerked about on her trembling knees the poor driven creature would have chosen ways of candor and gentleness. It was, strangely enough, only when I looked at Kitty and marked how her brightly colored prettiness arched over this plain criminal as though she were a splendid bird of prey and this her sluggish insect food that I felt the moment degrading.

Kitty was, I felt, being a little too clever over it.

"How is he wounded?" she asked.

The caller traced a pattern on the carpet with her blunt toe.

"I don't know how to put it; he's not exactly wounded. A shell burst—"

"Concussion?" suggested Kitty.

She answered with an odd glibness and humility, as though tendering us a term she had long brooded over without arriving at comprehension, and hoping that our superior intelligences would make something of it:

"Shell-shock." Our faces did not illumine, so she dragged on lamely, "Anyway, he's not well." Again she played with her purse. Her face was visibly damp.

"Not well? Is he dangerously ill?"

"Oh, no." She was too kind to harrow us. "Not dangerously ill."

Kitty brutally permitted a silence to fall. Our caller could not bear it, and broke it in a voice that nervousness had turned to a funny, diffident croak.

"He's in the Queen Mary Hospital at Boulogne." We did not speak, and she began to flush and wriggle on her seat, and stooped forward to fumble under the legs of her chair for her umbrella. The sight of its green seams and unveracious tortoiseshell handle disgusted Kitty into speech.

"How do you know all this?"

Our visitor met her eyes. This was evidently a moment for which she had steeled herself, and she rose to it with a catch of her breath. "A man who used to be a clerk along with my husband is in Mr. Baldry's regiment." Her voice croaked even more piteously, and her eyes begged: "Leave it at that! Leave it at that! If you only knew—"

"And what regiment is that?" pursued Kitty.

The poor sallow face shone with sweat.

"I never thought to ask," she said.

"Well, your friend's name—"

Mrs. Grey moved on her seat so suddenly and violently that the pigskin purse fell from her lap and lay at my feet. I supposed that she cast it from her purposely because its emptiness had brought her to this humiliation, and that the scene would close presently in a few quiet tears.

I hoped that Kitty would let her go without scarring her too much with words and would not mind if I gave her a little money. There was no doubt in my mind but that this queer, ugly episode in which this woman butted like a clumsy animal at a gate she was not intelligent enough to open would dissolve and be replaced by some more pleasing composition in which we would take our proper parts; in which, that is, she would turn from our rightness ashamed. Yet she cried:

"But Chris is ill!"

It took only a second for the compact insolence of the moment to penetrate, the amazing impertinence of the use of his name, the accusation of callousness she brought against us whose passion for Chris was our point of honor, because we would not shriek at her false news, the impudently bright, indignant gaze she flung at us, the lift of her voice that pretended she could not understand our coolness and irrelevance. I pushed the purse away from me with my toe, and hated her as the rich hate the poor as insect things that will struggle out of the crannies which are their decent home and introduce ugliness to the light of day. And Kitty said in a voice shaken with pitilessness:

"You are impertinent. I know exactly what you are doing. You have read in the 'Harrow Observer' or somewhere that my husband is at the front, and you come to tell this story because you think that you will get some money. I've read of such cases in the papers. You forget that if anything had happened to my husband the War Office would have told me. You should think yourself very lucky that I don't hand you over to the police." She shrilled a little before she came to the end. "Please go!"

"Kitty!" I breathed. I was so ashamed that such a scene should spring from Chris's peril at the front that I wanted to go out into the garden and sit by the pond until the poor thing had removed her deplorable umbrella, her unpardonable raincoat, her poor frustrated fraud. But Mrs. Grey, who had begun childishly and deliberately, "It's *you* who are being—" and had desisted simply because she realized that there were no harsh notes on her lyre, and that she could not strike these chords that others found so easy, had fixed me with a certain wet, clear, patient gaze. It is the gift of animals and those of peasant stock. From the least regarded, from an old horse nosing over a gate, or a drab in a work-house ward, it wrings the heart. From this woman—I said checkingly:

"Kitty!" and reconciled her in an undertone. "There's some mistake. Got the name wrong, perhaps. Please tell us all about it."

Mrs. Grey began a forward movement like a curtsy. She was groveling after that purse. When she rose, her face was pink from stooping, and her dignity swam uncertainly in a sea of half-shed tears. She said:

"I'm sorry I've upset you. But when you know a thing like that it isn't in flesh and blood to keep it from his wife. I am a married woman myself, and I know. I knew Mr. Baldry fifteen years ago." Her voice freely confessed that she had taken a liberty. "Quite a friend of the family he was." She had added that touch to soften the crude surprisingness of her announcement. It hardly did. "We lost sight of each other. It's fifteen years since we last met. I had never seen nor heard of him nor thought to do again till I got this a week ago."

She undid the purse and took out a telegram. I knew suddenly that all she said was true; for that was why her hands had clasped that purse.

"He isn't well! He isn't well!" she said pleadingly. "He's lost his memory, and thinks—thinks he still knows me."

She passed the telegram to Kitty, who read it, and laid it on her knee.

"See," said Mrs. Grey, "it's addressed to Margaret Allington, my maiden name, and I've been married these ten years. And it was sent to my old home, Monkey Island, at Bray. Father kept the inn there. It's fifteen years since we

13

left it. I never should have got this telegram if me and my husband hadn't been down there last September and told the folks who keep it now who I was."

Kitty folded up the telegram and said in a little voice: "This is a likely story."

Again Mrs. Grey's eyes brimmed. "People are rude to one," she visibly said, but surely not nice people like this. She simply continued to sit.

Kitty cried out, as though arguing:

"There's nothing about shell-shock in this wire."

Our visitor melted into a trembling shyness.

"There was a letter, too."

Kitty held out her hand.

She gasped:

"Oh, no, I couldn't do that!"

"I must have it," said Kitty.

The caller's eyes grew great. She rose and dived clumsily for her umbrella, which had again slipped under the chair.

"I can't," she cried, and scurried to the open door like a pelted dog. She would have run down the steps at once had not some tender thought arrested her. She turned to me trustfully and stammered, "He is at that hospital I said," as if, since I had dealt her no direct blow, I might be able to salve the news she brought from the general wreck of manners. And then Kitty's stiff pallor struck to her heart, and cried comfortingly across the distance, "I tell you, I haven't seen him for fifteen years." She faced about, pushed down her hat on her head, and ran down the steps to the gravel. "They won't understand!" we heard her sob.

For a long time we watched her as she went along the drive, her yellowish raincoat looking sick and bright in the sharp sunshine, her black plumes nodding like the pines above, her cheap boots making her walk on her heels, a spreading stain on the fabric of our life. When she was quite hidden by the dark clump of rhododendrons at the corner, Kitty turned and went to the fireplace. She laid her arms against the oak mantel-piece and cooled her face against her arms.

When at last I followed her she said:

"Do you believe her?"

I started. I had forgotten that we had ever disbelieved her.

"Yes," I replied.

"What can it mean?" She dropped her arms and stared at me imploringly. "Think, think, of something it can mean which isn't detestable!"

"It's all a mystery," I said; and added madly, because nobody had ever been cross with Kitty, "You didn't help to clear it up."

"Oh, I know you think I was rude," she petulantly moaned; "but you're so slow you don't see what it means. Either it means that he's mad, our Chris, our splendid, sane Chris, all broken and queer, not knowing us—I can't bear to think of that. It can't be true. But if he isn't—Jenny, there was nothing in that telegram to show he'd lost his memory. It was just affection—a name that might have been a pet name, things that it was a little common to put in a telegram. It's queer he should have written such a message, queer that he shouldn't have told me about knowing her, queer that he ever should have known such a woman. It shows there are bits of him we don't know. Things may be awfully wrong. It's all such a breach of trust! I resent it."

I was appalled by these stiff, dignified gestures that seemed to be plucking Chris's soul from his body, tormented though it was by this unknown calamity.

15

"But Chris is ill!" I cried.

She stared at me.

"You're saying what she said."

Indeed, there seemed no better words than those Mrs. Grey had used. I repeated:

"But he is ill!"

She laid her face against her arms again.

"What does that matter?" she wailed. "If he could send that telegram, he is no longer ours."

CHAPTER 2

I WAS sorry the next morning that the post comes too late at Harrowweald to be brought up with the morning tea and waits for one at the breakfast table; for under Kitty's fixed gaze I had to open a letter which bore the Boulogne postmark and was addressed in the writing of Frank Baldry, Chris's cousin, who is in the church. He wrote:

DEAR JENNY:

You will have to break it to Kitty and try to make her take it as quietly as possible. This sentence will sound ominous as a start, but I'm so full of the extraordinary thing that has happened to Chris that I feel as if every living creature was in possession of the facts. I don't know how much you know about it, so I'd better begin at the beginning. Last Thursday I got a wire from Chris, saying that he had had concussion, though not seriously, and was in a hospital about a mile from Boulogne, where he would be glad to see me. It struck me as odd that it had been sent to Ollenshaws, where I was curate fifteen years ago. Fortunately, I have always kept in touch with Sumpter, whom I regard as a specimen of the very best type of country clergymen, and he forwarded it without unnecessary delay. I started that evening, and looked hard for you and Kitty on the boat; but came to the conclusion I should probably find you at the hospital. After having breakfasted in the town,—how superior French cooking is! I would have looked in vain for such coffee, such an omelet, in my own parish,—I went off to look for the hospital. It is a girls' school, which has been taken over by the Red Cross, with fair-sized grounds and plenty of nice dry paths under the *tilleuls*. I could not see Chris for an hour, so I sat down on a bench by a funny, little round pond, with a stone coping, very French. Some wounded soldiers who came out to sit in the sun were rather rude because I was not in khaki, even when I explained that I was a priest of God and that the feeling of the bishops was strongly against the enlistment of the clergy. I do feel that the church has lost its grip on the masses.

Then a nurse came out and took me in to see Chris. He is in a nice room, with a southern exposure, with three other officers, who seemed very decent (not the "new army," I am glad to say). He was better than I had expected, but did not look quite himself. For one thing, he was oddly boisterous. He seemed glad to see me, and told me he could remember nothing about his concussion, but that he wanted to get back to Harrowweald. He talked a lot about the wood and the upper pond and wanted to know if the daffies were out yet, and when he would be allowed to travel, because he felt that he would get well at once if only he could get home. And then he was silent for a minute, as though he

18

was holding something back. It will perhaps help you to realize the difficulty of my position when you understand that all this happened before I had been in the room five minutes!

Without flickering an eyelid, quite easily and naturally, he gave me the surprising information that he was in love with a girl called Margaret Allington, who is the daughter of a man who keeps the inn on Monkey Island, at Bray on the Thames. He uttered some appreciations of this woman which I was too upset to note. I gasped, "How long has this been going on?" He laughed at my surprise, and said, "Ever since I went down to stay with Uncle Ambrose at Dorney after I'd got my B.Sc." Fifteen years ago! I was still staring at him, unable to believe this barefaced admission of a deception carried on for years, when he went on to say that, though he had wired to her and she had wired a message in return, she hadn't said anything about coming over to see him. "Now," he said quite coolly, "I know old Allington's had a bad season,—oh, I'm quite well up in the innkeeping business these days,—and I think it may quite possibly be a lack of funds that is keeping her away. I've lost my check-book somewhere in the scrim, and so I wonder if you'd send her some money. Or, better still, for she's a shy country thing, you might fetch her."

I stared. "Chris," I said, "I know the war is making some of us very lax, and I can only ascribe to that the shamelessness with which you admit the existence of a long-standing intrigue; but when it comes to asking me to go over to England and fetch the woman—" He interrupted me with a sneer that we parsons are inveterately eighteenth century and have our minds perpetually inflamed by visions of squires' sons seducing country wenches, and declared that he meant to marry this Margaret Allington. "Oh, indeed!" I said. "And may I ask what Kitty says to this arrangement?" "Who the devil is Kitty?" he asked blankly. "Kitty is your wife," I said quietly, but firmly. He sat up and shouted: "I haven't got a wife! Has some woman been turning up with a cock-and-bull story of being my wife? Because it's the damnedest lie!"

I determined to settle the matter by sharp, common-sense handling. "Chris," I said, "you have evidently lost your memory. You were married to Kitty Ellis at St. George's, Hanover Square, on the third, or it may have been the fourth"—you know my wretched memory for dates—"of February, in 1906." He turned very pale and asked what year this was. "1916," I told him. He fell back in a fainting condition. The nurse came, and said I had done it all right this time, so she at least seemed to have known that he required a rude awakening, although the doctor, a very nice man, Winchester and New, told me he had known nothing of Chris's delusions.

An hour later I was called back into the room. Chris was looking at himself in a hand-mirror, which he threw on the floor as I entered. "You are right," he said; "I'm not twenty-one, but thirty-six." He said he felt lonely and afraid, and that I must bring Margaret Allington to him at once or he would die. Suddenly he stopped raving and asked, "Is father all right?" I prayed for guidance, and answered, "Your father passed away twelve years ago." He said, "Good God! can't you say he *died*," and he turned over and lay with his back to me. I have never before seen a strong man weep, and it is indeed a terrible sight. He moaned a lot, and began to call for this Margaret. Then he turned over again and said, "Now tell us all about this Kitty that I've married." I told him she was a beautiful little woman, and mentioned that she had a charming and cultivated soprano voice. He said very fractiously: "I don't like little women, and I hate anybody, male or female, who sings. O God, I don't like this Kitty. Take her away!" And then he began to rave again about this woman. He said that he was consumed with desire for her and that he would never rest until he once more held her in his arms. I had no suspicion that Chris had this side to his nature, and it was almost a relief when he fainted again.

I have not seen him since, and it is evening; but I have had a long talk with the doctor, who says that he has satisfied himself that Chris is suffering from a loss of memory extending over a period of fifteen years. He says that though, of course, it will be an occasion of great trial to us all, he thinks that, in view of Chris's expressed longing for Harrowweald, he ought to be taken home, and advises me to make all arrangements for bringing him back some time next week. I hope I shall be upheld in this difficult enterprise.

In the meantime I leave it to you to prepare Kitty for this terrible shock. I could have wished it were a woman of a different type who was to see my poor cousin through these dark days, but convey to her my deepest sympathy. Indeed, I never realized the horror of warfare until I saw my cousin, of whose probity I am as firmly convinced as of my own wantonly repudiating his most sacred obligations.

Yours ever,
FRANK.

Over my shoulder Kitty muttered:

"And he always pretended he liked my singing." Then she gripped my arm and shrieked in a possessive fury: "Bring him home! Bring him home!"

So, a week later, they brought Chris home.

From breakfast-time that day the house was pervaded with a day-before-the-funeral feeling. Although all duties arising from the occasion had been performed, one could settle to nothing else. Chris was expected at one, but then there came a telegram to say he was delayed till the late afternoon. So Kitty, whose beauty was as changed in grief from its ordinary seeming as a rose in moonlight is different from a rose by day, took me down after lunch to the greenhouses and had a snappishly competent conversation about the year's vegetables with Pipe, the gardener. Then Kitty went into the drawing-room and filled the house with the desolate merriment of an inattentively played pianola, while I sat in the hall and wrote letters and noticed how sad dance-music has sounded ever since the war began.

After that she started a savage raid of domestic efficiency, and made the housemaids cry because the brass handles of the tall-boys were not bright enough and because there was only ten-to-one instead of a hundred-to-one risk of breaking a leg on the parquet. Then she had tea, and hated the soda-cake. She was a little, shrunk thing, huddled in the arm-chair farthest from the light, when at last the big car came nosing up the drive through the dark.

We stood up. Through the thudding of the engines came the sound of Chris's great male voice which always had in it a note like the baying of a big dog. "Thanks, I can manage by myself." I heard, amazed, his step ring strong upon the stone, for I had felt his absence as a kind of death from which he would emerge ghostlike, impalpable. And then he stood in the doorway, the gloom blurring his outlines like fur, the faint, clear candle-light catching the fair down on his face. He did not see me, in my dark dress, or huddled Kitty, and with the sleepy smile of one who returns to a dear, familiar place to rest he walked into the hall and laid down his stick and his khaki cap beside the candlestick on the oak table. With both hands he felt the old wood, and stood humming happily through his teeth.

I cried out, because I had seen that his hair was of three colors now, brown and gold and silver.

With a quick turn of the head, he found me out in the shadows.

"Hullo, Jenny!" he said, and gripped my hands.

"O Chris, I am so glad!" I stuttered, and then could say no more for shame that I was thirty-five instead of twenty. For his eyes had hardened in the midst of his welcome, as though he had trusted that I at least would have been no party to this conspiracy to deny that he was young, and he said:

23

"I've dropped Frank in town. My temper's of the convalescent type." He might as well have said, "I've dropped Frank, who had grown old, like you."

"Chris," I went on, "it's so wonderful to have you safe."

"Safe," he repeated. He sighed very deeply and continued to hold my hands. There was a rustle in the shadows, and he dropped my hands.

The face that looked out of the dimness to him was very white, and her upper lip was lifted over her teeth in a distressed grimace. It was immediately as plain as though he had shouted it that this sad mask meant nothing to him. He knew not because memory had given him any insight into her heart, but because there is an instinctive kindliness in him which makes him wise about all suffering, that it would hurt her if he asked if this was his wife; but his body involuntarily began a gesture of inquiry before he realized that that, too, would hurt her, and he checked it half-way. So, through a silence, he stood before her slightly bent, as though he had been maimed.

"I am your wife." There was a weak, wailing anger behind the words.

"Kitty," he said softly and kindly. He looked around for some graciousness to make the scene less wounding, and stooped to kiss her; but he could not. The thought of another woman made him unable to breathe, sent the blood running under his skin.

With a toss, like a child saying, "Well, if you don't want to, I'm sure I wouldn't for the world!" Kitty withdrew from the suspended caress. He watched her retreat into the shadows as though she were a symbol of this new life by which he was baffled and oppressed, until the darkness outside became filled with the sound like the surf which we always hear at Harrowweald on angry evenings, and his eyes became distant, and his lips smiled. "Up here—in this old place—how one hears the pines!"

She cried out from the other end of the room, as though she were speaking with some one behind a shut door:

"I've ordered dinner at seven. I thought you'd probably have missed a meal or two, or would want to go to bed early." She said it very smartly, with her head on one side like a bird, as if she was pleading that he would find her very clever about ordering dinner and thinking of his comfort.

"Good," he said. "I'd better dress now, hadn't I?" He looked up the stair-case, and would have gone up had I not held him back; for the little room in the south wing, with the fishing-rods and the old books, went in the rebuilding, absorbed by the black-and-white magnificence that is Kitty's bedroom.

"Oh, I'll take you up," Kitty rang out efficiently. She pulled at his coat-sleeve, so they started level on the lowest step. But as they went up, the sense of his separateness beat her back; she lifted her arms as though she struggled through a fog, and fell behind. When he reached the top she was standing half-way down the stairs, her hands clasped under her chin. But he did not see her. He was looking along the corridor and saying, "This house is different." If the soul has to stay in its coffin till the lead is struck asunder, in its captivity it speaks with such a voice.

She braced herself with a gallant laugh.

"How you've forgotten!" she cried, and ran up to him, rattling her keys and looking grave with housewifery, and I was left alone with the dusk and the familiar things. The dusk flowed in wet and cool from the garden, as if to put out the fire of confusion lighted on our hearthstone, and the furniture, very visible through that soft evening opacity with the observant brightness of old, well-polished wood, seemed terribly aware. Strangeness had come into the house, and everything was appalled by it, even time. For the moments dragged. It seemed to me, half an hour later, that I had been standing for an infinite period in the drawing-room, remembering that in the old days the blinds had never been drawn in this room because old Mrs. Baldry had liked to see the night gathering like a pool in the valley while the day lingered as a white streak above the farthest hills, and perceiving in pain that the heavy blue blinds that shroud the nine windows because a lost Zeppelin sometimes clanks like a skeleton across the sky above us would make his home seem even more like prison.

I began to say what was in my mind to Kitty when she came in, but she moved past me, remote in preoccupation, and I was silent when I saw that she was dressed in all respects like a bride. The gown she wore on her wedding-day ten years ago had been cut and embroidered as this white satin was; her hair had been coiled low on her neck, as it was now. Around her throat were her pearls, and her longer chain of diamonds dropped, looking cruelly bright, to her white, small breasts; because she held some needlework to her bosom, I saw that her right hand was stiff with rings and her left hand bare save for her wedding-ring. She dropped her load of flannel on a work-table and sat down, spreading out her skirts, in an arm-chair by the fire. With her lower lip thrust out, as if she were considering a menu, she lowered her head and looked down on herself. She frowned to see that the high lights on the satin shone scarlet from the fire, that her flesh glowed like a rose, and she changed her seat for a high-backed chair beneath the farthest candle-sconce. There were green curtains close by, and now the lights on her satin gown were green like cleft ice. She looked as cold as moonlight, as virginity, but

26

precious; the falling candle-light struck her hair to bright, pure gold. So she waited for him.

There came suddenly a thud at the door. We heard Chris swear and stumble to his feet, while one of the servants spoke helpfully. Kitty knitted her brows, for she hates gracelessness, and a failure of physical adjustment is the worst indignity she can conceive.

"He's fallen down those three steps from the hall," I whispered. "They're new." She did not listen, because she was controlling her face into harmony with the appearance of serene virginity upon which his eyes would fall when he entered the room.

His fall had ruffled him and made him look very large and red, and he breathed hard, like an animal pursued into a strange place by night, and to his hot consciousness of his disorder the sight of Kitty, her face and hands and bosom shining like the snow, her gown enfolding her, and her gold hair crowning her with radiance, and the white fire of jewels giving passion to the spectacle, was a deep refreshment. She sat still for a time, so that he might feel this well, then raised her ringed hand to her necklaces.

"It seems so strange that you should not remember me," she said. "You gave me all these."

He answered kindly:

"I am glad I did that. You look very beautiful in them." But as he spoke his gaze shifted to the shadows in the corners of the room, and the blood ran hot under his skin. He was thinking of another woman, of another beauty.

Kitty put up her hands as if to defend her jewels.

In that silence dinner was announced, and we went into the dining-room. It is the fashion at Baldry Court to use no electric light save when there is work to be done or a great company to be entertained, and to eat and talk by

27

the mild clarity of many candles. That night it was a kindly fashion, for we sat about the table with our faces veiled in shadow, and seemed to listen in quiet contentment to the talk of our man who had come back to us. Yet all through the meal I was near to weeping, because whenever he thought himself unobserved he looked at the things that were familiar to him. Dipping his head, he would glance sidewise at the old oak paneling, and nearer things he fingered as though sight were not intimate enough a contact. His hand caressed the arm of his chair, because he remembered the black gleam of it, stole out and touched the recollected salt-cellar. It was his furtiveness that was heartrending; it was as though he were an outcast, and we who loved him stout policemen. Was Baldry Court so sleek a place that the unhappy felt offenders there? Then we had all been living wickedly, and he, too. As his fingers glided here and there he talked bravely about non-committal things: to what ponies we had been strapped when at the age of five we were introduced to the hunting-field; how we had teased to be allowed to keep swans in the pond above the wood, and how the yellow bills of our intended pets had sent us shrieking homeward; and all the dear life that makes the bland English country-side secretly adventurous. "Funny thing," he said. "All the time I was at Boulogne I wanted to see a kingfisher, that blue scudding down a stream, or a heron's flight round a willow—" He checked himself suddenly; his head fell forward on his chest. "You have no herons here, of course," he said drearily, and fingered the arm of his chair again. Then he raised his head again, brisk with another subject. "Do they still have trouble with foxes at Steppy End?"

Kitty shook her head.

"I don't know."

"Griffiths will know," Chris said cheerily, and swung round on his seat to ask the butler, and found him osseous, where Griffiths was rotund; dark, where Griffiths had been merrily mottled; strange, where Griffiths had been a part of home, a condition of life. He sat back in his chair as though his heart had stopped.

When the butler who is not Griffiths had left the room he spoke gruffly.

"Stupid of me, I know; but where is Griffiths?"

"Dead seven years ago," said Kitty, her eyes on her plate.

He sighed deeply in a shuddering horror.

"I'm sorry. He was a good man."

I cleared my throat.

"There are new people here, Chris, but they love you as the old ones did."

He forced himself to smile at us both, to a gay response.

"As if I didn't know that to-night!"

But he did not know it. Even to me he would give no trust, because it was Jenny the girl who had been his friend and not Jenny the woman. All the inhabitants at this new tract of time were his enemies, all its circumstances his prison-bars. There was suspicion in the gesture with which, when we were back in the drawing-room he picked up the flannel from the work-table.

"Whose is this?" he said curiously. His mother had been a hard-riding woman, not apt with her needle.

"Clothes for one of the cottages," answered Kitty, breathlessly. "We—we've a lot of responsibilities, you and I. With all of the land you've bought, there are ever so many people to look after."

He moved his shoulders uneasily, as if under a yoke, and, after he had drunk his coffee, pulled up one of the blinds and went out to pace the flagged walk under the windows. Kitty huddled carelessly by the fire, her hands over her face, unheeding by its red glow she looked not so virginal and bride-like; so I think she was too distracted even to plan. I went to the piano. Through this evening of sentences cut short because their completed meaning was always sorrow, of normal life dissolved to tears, the chords of Beethoven sounded serenely.

"So you like Jenny," said Kitty, suddenly, "to play Beethoven when it's the war that's caused all this. I could have told that you would have chosen to play German music this night of all nights."

So I began a saraband by Purcell, a jolly thing that makes one see a plump, sound woman dancing on a sanded floor in some old inn, with casks of good ale all about her and a world of sunshine and May lanes without. As I played I wondered if things like this happened when Purcell wrote such music, empty of everything except laughter and simple greeds and satisfactions and at worst the wail of unrequited love. Why had modern life brought forth these horrors, which made the old tragedies seem no more than nursery-shows? And the sky also is different. Behind Chris's head, as he halted at the open window, a search-light turned all ways in the night, like a sword brandished among the stars.

"Kitty."

"Yes, Chris." She was sweet and obedient and alert.

"I know my conduct must seem to you perversely insulting,"—behind him the search-light wheeled while he gripped the sides of the window,—"but if I do not see Margaret Allington I shall die."

She raised her hands to her jewels, and pressed the cool globes of her pearls into her flesh. "She lives near here," she said easily. "I will send the car down for her to-morrow. You shall see as much of her as you like."

His arms fell to his sides.

"Thank you," he muttered; "you're all being so kind—"
He disengaged himself into the darkness.

I was amazed at Kitty's beautiful act and more amazed
to find that it had made her face ugly. Her eyes snapped as
they met mine.

"That dowd!" she said, keeping her voice low, so that
he might not hear it as he passed to and fro before the
window. "That dowd!"

This sudden abandonment of beauty and amiability
meant so much in our Kitty, whose law of life is grace, that
I went over and kissed her.

"Dear, you're taking things all the wrong way," I said.
"Chris is ill—"

"He's well enough to remember her all right," she replied
unanswerably. Her silver shoe tapped the floor; she pinched
her lips for some moments. "After all, I suppose I can sit
down to it. Other women do. Teddy Rex keeps a Gaiety
girl, and Mrs. Rex has to grin and bear it." She shrugged
in answer to my silence. "What else is it, do you think? It
means that Chris is a man like other men. But I did think
that bad women were pretty. I suppose he's had so much
to do with pretty ones that a plain one's a change."

"Kitty! Kitty! how can you!"

But her little pink mouth went on manufacturing mal-
ice.

"This is all a blind," she said at the end of an unpardonable sentence. "He's pretending."

I, who had felt his agony all the evening like a wound
in my own body, was past speech then, and I did not care
what I did to stop her. I gripped her small shoulders with
my large hands, and shook her till her jewels rattled and
she scratched my fingers and gasped for breath. But I did

not mind so long as she was silent.

Chris spoke from the darkness.

"Jenny!" I let her go. He came in and stood over us, running his hand through his hair unhappily. "Let's all be decent to each other," he said heavily. "It's all such a muddle, and it's so rotten for all of us—"

Kitty shook herself neat and stood up.

"Why don't you say, 'Jenny, you mustn't be rude to visitors'? It's how you feel, I know." She gathered up her needlework. "I'm going to bed. It's been a horrid night."

She spoke so pathetically, like a child who hasn't enjoyed a party as much as it had thought it would, that both of us felt a stir of tenderness toward her as she left the room. We smiled sadly at each other as we sat down by the fire, and I perceived that, perhaps because I was flushed and looked younger, he felt more intimate with me than he had yet done since his return. Indeed, in the warm, friendly silence that followed he was like a patient when tiring visitors have gone and he is left alone with his trusted nurse; smiled under drooped lids and then paid me the high compliment of disregard. His limbs relaxed, he sank back into his chair. I watched him vigilantly, and was ready at that moment when thought intruded into his drowsings and his face began to twitch. I asked:

"You can't remember her at all?"

"Oh, yes," he said, without raising his eyelids, "in a sense. I know how she bows when you meet her in the street, how she dresses when she goes to church. I know her as one knows a woman staying in the same hotel, just like that."

"It's a pity you can't remember Kitty. All that a wife should be she's been to you."

He sat forward, warming his palms at the blaze and hunching his shoulders as though there were a draft. His silence compelled me to look at him, and I found his eyes, cold and incredulous and frightened, on me.

"Jenny, is this true?"

"That Kitty's been a good wife?"

"That Kitty is my wife, that I am old, that"—he waved a hand at the altered room—"all this."

"It is all true. She is your wife, and this place is changed, and it's better and jollier in all sorts of ways, believe me, and fifteen years have passed. Why, Chris, can't you see that I have grown old?" My vanity could hardly endure his slow stare, but I kept my fingers clasped on my lap. "You see?"

He turned away with an assenting mutter; but I saw that deep down in him, not to be moved by any material proof, his spirit was incredulous.

"Tell me what seems real to you," I begged. "Chris, be a pal. I'll never tell."

"M-m-m," he said. His elbows were on his knees, and his hands stroked his thick tarnished hair. I could not see his face, but I knew that his skin was red and that his gray eyes were wet and bright. Then suddenly he lifted his chin and laughed, like a happy swimmer breaking through a wave that has swept him far inshore. He glowed with a radiance that illuminated the moment till my blood tingled and I began to rub my hands together and laugh, too. "Why, Monkey Island's real. But you don't know old Monkey. Let me tell you."

CHAPTER 3

CHRIS told the story lingeringly, in loving detail. From Uncle Ambrose's gates, it seems, one took the path across the meadow where Whiston's cows are put to graze, passed through the second stile—the one between the two big alders—into a long straight road that ran across the flat lands to Bray. After a mile or so there branched from it a private road that followed a line of noble poplars down to the ferry. Between two of them—he described it meticulously, as though it were of immense significance—there stood a white hawthorn. In front were the dark-green, glassy waters of an unvisited back-water, and beyond them a bright lawn set with many walnut-trees and a few great chestnuts, well lighted with their candles, and to the left of that a low, white house with a green dome rising in its middle, and a veranda with a roof of hammered iron that had gone verdigris-color with age and the Thames weather. This was the Monkey Island Inn. The third Duke of Marlborough had built it for a "folly," and perching there with nothing but a line of walnut-trees and a fringe of lawn between it and the fast, full, shining Thames, it had an eighteenth-century grace and silliness.

Well, one sounded the bell that hung on a post, and presently Margaret in a white dress would come out of the porch and would walk to the stone steps down to the river. Invariably, as she passed the walnut-tree that overhung the path, she would pick a leaf, crush it, and sniff the sweet

34

scent; and as she came near the steps she would shade her eyes and peer across the water. "She is a little near-sighted; you can't imagine how sweet it makes her look," Chris explained. (I did not say that I had seen her, for, indeed, this Margaret I had never seen.) A sudden serene gravity would show that she had seen one, and she would get into the four-foot punt that was used as a ferry and bring it over very slowly, with rather stiff movements of her long arms, to exactly the right place. When she had got the punt up on the gravel her serious brow would relax, and she would smile at one and shake hands and say something friendly, like, "Father thought you'd be over this afternoon, it being so fine; so he's saved some duck's eggs for tea."

And then one took the pole from her and brought her back to the island, though probably one did not mount the steps to the lawn for a long time. It was so good to sit in the punt by the landing-stage while Margaret dabbled her hands in the black waters and forgot her shyness as one talked. "She's such good company. She's got an accurate mind that would have made her a good engineer, but when she picks up facts she kind of gives them a motherly hug. She's charity and love itself." (Again I did not say that I had seen her.) If people drifted in to tea, one had to talk to her while she cut the bread and butter and the sandwiches in the kitchen, but in this year of floods few visitors cared to try the hard rowing below Bray Lock.

So usually one sat down there in the boat, talking with a sense of leisure, as though one had all the rest of one's life in which to carry on this conversation, and noting how the reflected ripple of the water made a bright, vibrant, mark upon her throat, and other effects of the scene upon her beauty, until the afternoon grew drowsy, and she said, "Father will be wanting his tea." And they would go up and find old Allington, in white ducks, standing in the fringe of long grasses and cow-parsley on the other edge of the island, looking to his poultry or his rabbits. He was a little man, with a tuft of copper-colored hair rising from the middle of his forehead like a clown's curl, who shook hands hard and explained very soon that he was a rough diamond.

Then they all had tea under the walnut-tree where the canary's cage was hanging, and the ducks' eggs would be brought out, and Mr. Allington would talk much Thames-side gossip: how the lock-keeper at Teddington had had his back broken by a swan, mad as swans are in May; how they would lose their license at the Dovetail Arms if they were not careful; and how the man who kept the inn by Surly Hall was like to die, because after he had been cursing his daughter for two days for having run away with a soldier from Windsor Barracks, he had suddenly seen her white face in a clump of rushes in the river just under the hole in the garden fence. Margaret would sit quiet, round-eyed at the world's ways, and shy because of Chris.

So they would sit on that bright lawn until the day was dyed with evening blue, and Mr. Allington was more and more often obliged to leap into the punt to chase his ducks, which had started on a trip to Bray Lock, or to crawl into the undergrowth after rabbits similarly demoralized by the dusk.

Then Chris would say he had to go, and they would stand in a communing silence while the hearty voice of Mr. Allington shouted from midstream or under the alder-boughs a disregarded invitation to stay and have a bite of supper. In the liquefaction of colors which happens on a summer evening, when the green grass seemed like a precious fluid poured out on the earth and dripping over to the river, and the chestnut candles were no longer proud flowers, but just wet, white lights in the humid mass of the tree, when the brown earth seemed just a little denser than the water, Margaret also participated.

Chris explained this part of his story stumblingly; but I, too, have watched people I loved in the dusk, and I know what he meant. As she sat in the punt while he ferried himself across it was no longer visible that her fair hair curled differently and that its rather wandering parting was a little on one side; that her straight brows, which were a little darker than her hair, were nearly always contracted in a frown of conscientious speculation; that her mouth and chin were noble, yet as delicate as flowers; that her shoulders were slightly hunched because her young body, like a lily-stem, found it difficult to manage its own tallness. She was then just a girl in white who lifted a white face or drooped a dull-gold head. Then she was nearer to him than at any other time. That he loved her in this twilight, which obscured all the physical details which he adored, seemed to him a guarantee that theirs was a changeless love which would persist if she were old or maimed or disfigured.

He stood beside the crazy post where the bell hung and watched the white figure take the punt over the black waters, mount the gray steps, and assume some of their grayness, become a green shade in the green darkness of the foliage-darkened lawn, and he exulted in that guarantee.

How long this went on he had forgotten; but it continued for some time before there came the end of his life, the last day he could remember. I was barred out of that day. His lips told me of its physical appearances, while from his wet, bright eyes and his flushed skin, his beautiful signs of a noble excitement, I tried to derive the real story. It seemed that the day when he bicycled over to Monkey Island, happy because Uncle Ambrose had gone up to town and he could stay to supper with the Allingtons, was the most glorious day the year had yet brought. The whole world seemed melting into light. Cumulus-clouds floated very high, like lumps of white light, against a deep, glowing sky, and dropped dazzling reflections on the beaming Thames. The trees moved not like timber, shocked by wind, but floatingly, like weeds at the bottom of a well of sunshine. When Margaret came out of the porch and paused, as she always did, to crush and smell the walnut-leaf and shade her eyes with her hand, her white dress shone like silver.

She brought the punt across and said very primly, "Dad will be disappointed; he's gone up to town on business," and answered gravely, "That is very kind of you," when he took the punt-pole from her and said laughingly: "Never mind. I'll come and see you all the same." (I could see them as Chris spoke, so young and pale and solemn, with the intense light spilling all around them.) That afternoon they did not sit in the punt by the landing-stage, but wandered about the island and played with the rabbits and looked at the ducks and were inordinately silent. For a long time they stood in the fringe of rough grass on the other side of the island, and Margaret breathed contentedly that the Thames was so beautiful. Past the spit of sand at the far end of the island, where a great swan swanked to the empty reach that it would protect its mate against all comers, the river opened to a silver breadth between flat meadows stretching back to far rows of pin-thick black poplars, until it wound away to Windsor behind a line of high trees whose heads were bronze with unopened buds, and whose flanks were hidden by a head of copper-beech and crimson and

38

white hawthorn.

Chris said he would take her down to Dorney Lock in the skiff, and she got in very silently and obediently; but as soon as they were out in midstream she developed a sense of duty, and said she could not leave the inn with just that boy to look after it. And then she went into the kitchen and, sucking in her lower lip for shyness, very conscientiously cut piles of bread and butter in case some visitors came to tea. Just when Chris was convincing her of the impossibility of any visitors arriving they came, a fat woman in a luscious pink blouse and an old chap who had been rowing in a tweed waistcoat. Chris went out, though Margaret laughed and trembled and begged him not to, and waited on them. It should have been a great lark, but suddenly he hated them, and when they offered him a tip for pushing the boat off, he snarled absurdly and ran back, miraculously relieved, to the bar-parlor.

Still Margaret would not leave the island. "Supposing," she said, "that Mr. Learoyd comes for his ale." But she consented to walk with him to the wild part of the island, where poplars and alders and willows grew round a clearing in which white willow-herb and purple figwort and here and there a potato-flower, last ailing consequence of one of Mr. Allington's least successful enterprises, fought down to the fringe of iris on the river's lip. In this gentle jungle was a rustic seat, relic of a reckless aspiration on the part of Mr. Allington to make this a pleasure-garden, and on it they sat until a pale moon appeared above the green corn-field on the other side of the river. "Not six yet," he said, taking out his watch. "Not six yet," she repeated. Words seemed to bear more significance than they had ever borne before. Then a heron flapped gigantic in front of the moon, and swung in wide circles round the willow-tree before them.

"Oh, look!" she cried. He seized the hand she flung upward and gathered her into his arms. They were so for long, while the great bird's wings beat about them.

Afterward she pulled at his hand. She wanted to go back across the lawn and walk round the inn, which looked mournful, as unlit houses do by dusk. They passed beside the green-and-white stucco barrier of the veranda and stood on the three-cornered lawn that shelved high over the stream at the island's end, regarding the river, which was now something more wonderful than water, because it had taken to its bosom the rose and amber glories of the sunset smoldering behind the elms and Bray church-tower. Birds sat on the telegraph wires that spanned the river as the black notes sit on a staff of music. Then she went to the window of the parlor and rested her cheek against the glass, looking in. The little room was sad with twilight, and there was nothing to be seen but Margaret's sewing-machine on the table and the enlarged photograph of Margaret's mother over the mantel-piece, and the views of Tintern Abbey framed in red plush, and on the floor, the marigold pattern making itself felt through the dusk, Mr. Allington's carpet slippers. "Think of me sitting in there," she whispered, "not knowing you loved me." Then they went into the bar and drank milk, while she walked about fingering familiar things with an absurd expression of exaltation, as though that day she was fond of everything, even the handles of the beer-engine.

When there had descended on them a night as brilliant as the day he drew her out into the darkness, which was sweet with the scent of walnut-leaves, and they went across the lawn, bending beneath the chestnut-boughs, not to the wild part of the island, but to a circle of smooth turf divided from it by a railing of wrought iron. On this stood a small Greek temple, looking very lovely in the moonlight. He had never brought Margaret here before, because Mr. Allington had once told him, spatulate forefinger at his nose, that it had been built for the "dook" for his excesses, and it was in the quality of his love for her that he could not bear to think of her in association with anything base. But to-night there was nothing anywhere but beauty. He lifted her in his arms and carried her within the columns, and made her stand in a niche above the altar. A strong stream of moonlight rushed upon her there; by its light he could not tell if her hair was white as silver or yellow as gold, and again he was filled with exaltation because he knew that it would not have mattered if it had been white. His love was changeless. Lifting her down from the niche, he told her so.

And as he spoke, her warm body melted to nothingness in his arms. The columns that had stood so hard and black against the quivering tide of moonlight and starlight seemed to totter and dissolve. He was lying in a hateful world where barbed-wire entanglements showed impish knots against a livid sky full of blooming noise and splashes of fire and wails for water, and his back was hurting intolerably.

Chris fell to blowing out the candles, and I, perhaps because the egotistical part of me was looking for something to say that would make him feel me devoted and intimate, could not speak.

Suddenly he desisted, stared at a candle-flame, and said:

"If you had seen the way she rested her cheek against the glass and looked into the little room you'd understand that I can't say, 'Yes, Kitty's my wife, and Margaret somehow just nothing at all.'"

"Of course you can't," I murmured sympathetically.

41

We gripped hands, and he brought down on our conversation the finality of darkness.

CHAPTER 4

NEXT morning it appeared that the chauffeur had taken the car up to town to get a part replaced, and Margaret could not be brought from Wealdstone till the afternoon. It fell to me to fetch her. "At least," Kitty had said, "I might be spared that humiliation." Before I started I went to the pond on the hill's edge. It is a place where autumn lives for half the year, for even when the spring lights tongues of green fire in the undergrowth, and the valley shows sunlit between the tree-trunks, here the pond is fringed with yellow bracken and tinted bramble, and the water flows amber over last winter's leaves.

Through this brown gloom, darkened now by a surly sky, Chris was taking the skiff, standing in the stern and using his oar like a gondolier. He had come down here soon after breakfast, driven from the house by the strangeness of all but the outer walls, and discontented with the grounds because everything but this wet, intractable spot bore the marks of Kitty's genius. After lunch there had been another attempt to settle down, but with a grim glare at a knot of late Christmas roses bright in a copse that fifteen years ago had been dark he went back to the russet-eaved boat-house and this play with the skiff. It was a boy's sport, and it was dreadful to see him turn a middle-aged face as he brought the boat inshore.

"I'm just going down to fetch Margaret," I said.

He thanked me for it.

43

"But, Chris, I must tell you. I've seen Margaret. She came up here, so kind and sweet, to tell us you were wounded. She's the greatest dear in the world, but she's not as you think of her. She's old, Chris. She isn't beautiful any longer. She's drearily married. She's seamed and scored and ravaged by squalid circumstances. You can't love her when you see her."

"Didn't I tell you last night," he said, "that that doesn't matter?" He dipped his oar to a stroke that sent him away from me. "Bring her soon. I shall wait for her down here."

Wealdstone is not, in its way, a bad place; it lies in the lap of open country, and at the end of every street rise the green hills of Harrow and the spires of Harrow School. But all the streets are long and red and freely articulated with railway arches, and factories spoil the skyline with red, angular chimneys, and in front of the shops stood little women with backs ridged by cheap stays, who tapped their upper lips with their forefingers and made other feeble, doubtful gestures, as though they wanted to buy something and knew that if they did they would have to starve some other appetite. When we asked them the way they turned to us faces sour with thrift. It was a town of people who could not do as they liked.

And here Margaret lived in a long road of red-brick boxes, flecked here and there with the pink blur of almond-blossom, which debouched in a flat field where green grass rose up rank through clay mold blackened by coal-dust from the railway. Mariposa, which was the last house in the road, did not even have an almond-tree. In the front garden, which seemed to be imperfectly reclaimed from the greasy field, yellow crocus and some sodden squills just winked, and the back, where a man was handling a spade without mastery, presented the austere appearance of an allotment. And not only did Margaret live in this place; she also belonged to it. When she opened the door she gazed at me with watering eyes, and in perplexity stroked her disordered hair with a floury hand. Her face was sallow with heat, and beads of perspiration glittered in the deep, dragging line between her nostrils and the corners of her mouth. She said:

"He's home?"

I nodded.

She pulled me inside and slammed the door.

"Is he well?" she asked.

"Quite," I answered.

Her tense stare relaxed. She rubbed her hands on her overall and said:

"You'll excuse me. It's the girl's day out. If you'll step into the parlor—"

So in her parlor I sat and told her how it was with Chris and how greatly he desired to see her. And as I spoke of his longing I turned my eyes away from her, because she was sitting on a sofa, upholstered in velveteen of a sickish green, which was so low that her knees stuck up in front of her, and she had to clasp them with her seamed, floury hands. I could see that the skin of her face was damp. And my voice failed me as I looked round the room, because I saw just what Margaret had seen that evening fifteen years ago when she had laid her cheek to the parlor window at Monkey Island. There was the enlarged photograph of Margaret's mother over the mantelpiece, on the walls were the views of Tintern Abbey framed in red plush, between the rickety legs of the china cupboard was the sewing-machine, and tucked into the corner between my chair and the fender were a pair of carpet slippers. All her life long Margaret, who in her time had partaken of the supreme dignity of a requited love, had lived with men who wore carpet slippers in the house. I turned my eyes away again, and this time looked down the garden at the figure that was not so much digging as exhibiting his incapacity to deal with a spade. He was sneezing very frequently, and his sneezes made the unbuckled straps at the back of his waistcoat wag violently. I supposed him to be Mr. William Grey.

I had finished the statement of our sad case, and I saw that though she had not moved, clasping her knees in a set, hideous attitude, the tears were rolling down her cheeks.

"Oh, don't! Oh, don't!" I exclaimed, standing up. Her tear-stained immobility touched the heart. "He's not so bad; he'll get quite well."

"I know, I know," she said miserably. "I don't believe that anything bad could be allowed to happen to Chris for long. And I'm sure," she said kindly, "you're looking after him beautifully. But when a thing you had thought had ended fifteen years ago starts all over again, and you're very tired—" She drew a hand across her tears, her damp skin, her rough, bagging overall. "I'm hot. I've been baking. You can't get a girl nowadays that understands the baking." Her gaze became remote and tender, and she said in a manner that was at once argumentative and narrative, as though she were telling the whole story to a neighbor over the garden wall: "I suppose I ought to say that he isn't right in his head, and that I'm married, so we'd better not meet; but, oh," she cried, and I felt as though, after much fumbling with damp matches and many doubts as to whether there was any oil in the wick, I had lit the lamp at last, "I want to see him so! It's wrong, I know it's wrong, but I am so glad Chris wants to see me, too!"

"You'll do him good." I found myself raising my voice

to the pitch she had suddenly attained as though to keep her at it. "Come now!"

She dipped suddenly to compassion.

"But the young lady?" she asked timidly. "She was upset the last time. I've often wondered if I did right in going. Even if Chris has forgotten, he'll want to do what's right. He couldn't bear to hurt her."

"That's true," I said. "You do know our Chris. He watches her out of the corner of his eye, even when he's feeling at his worst, to see she isn't wincing. But she sent me here to-day."

"Oh!" cried Margaret, glowing, "she must have a lovely nature!"

I lost suddenly the thread of the conversation. I could not talk about Kitty. She appeared to me at that moment a faceless figure with flounces, just as most of the servants at Baldry Court appear to me as faceless figures with caps and aprons. There were only two real people in the world, Chris and this woman whose personality was sounding through her squalor like a beautiful voice singing in a darkened room, and I was absorbed in a mental vision of them. You know how the saints and the prophets are depicted in the steel engravings in old Bibles; so they were standing, in flowing white robes on rocks against a pitch-black sky, a strong light beating on their eyes upturned in ecstasy and their hand outstretched to receive the spiritual blessing of which the fierce rays were an emanation. Into that rapt silence I desired to break, and I whispered irrelevantly, "Oh, nothing, nothing is too good for Chris!" while I said to myself, "If she really were like that, solemn and beatified!" and my eyes returned to look despairingly on her ugliness. But she really was like that. She had responded to my irrelevant murmur of adoration by just such a solemn and beatified appearance as I had imagined. Her grave eyes were upturned, her worn hands lay palm upward on her knees, as though to receive the love of which her radiance was an emanation. And then, at a sound in the kitchen, she snatched my exaltation from me by suddenly turning dull.

"I think that's Mr. Grey come in from his gardening. You'll excuse me."

Through the open door I heard a voice saying in a way which suggested that its production involved much agitation of a prominent Adam's apple:

"Well, dear, seeing you had a friend, I thought I'd better slip up and change my gardening trousers." I do not know what she said to him, but her voice was soft and comforting and occasionally girlish and interrupted by laughter, and I perceived from its sound that with characteristic gravity she had accepted it as her mission to keep loveliness and excitement alive in his life.

"An old friend of mine has been wounded," was the only phrase I heard; but when she drew him out into the garden under the window she had evidently explained the situation away, for he listened docilely as she said: "I've made some rock-cakes for your tea. And if I'm late for supper, there's a dish of macaroni cheese you must put in the oven and a tin of tomatoes to eat with it. And there is a little rhubarb and shape." She told them off on her fingers, and then whisked him round and buckled the wagging straps at the back of his waistcoat. He was a lank man, with curly gray hairs growing from every place where it is inadvisable that hairs should grow,—from the inside of his ears, from his nostrils, on the back of his hands,—but he looked pleased when she touched him, and he said in a devoted way:

"Very well, dear. Don't worry about me. I'll trot along

after tea and have a game of draughts with Brown."

She answered:

"Yes, dear. And now get on with those cabbages. You're going to keep me in lovely cabbages, just as you did last year, won't you, darling?" She linked arms with him and took him back to his digging.

When she came back into the parlor again she was wearing that yellowish raincoat, that hat with hearse plumes nodding over its sticky straw, that gray alpaca skirt. I first defensively clenched my hands. It would have been such agony to the finger-tips to touch any part of her apparel. And then I thought of Chris, to whom a second before I had hoped to bring a serene comforter. I perceived clearly that that ecstatic woman lifting her eyes and her hands to the benediction of love was Margaret as she existed in eternity; but this was Margaret as she existed in time, as the fifteen years between Monkey Island and this damp day in Ladysmith Road had irreparably made her. Well, I had promised to bring her to him.

She said:

"I'm ready," and against that simple view of her condition I had no argument. But when she paused by the painted drainpipe in the hall and peered under contracted brows for that unveracious tortoiseshell handle, I said hastily:

"Oh, don't trouble about an umbrella."

"I'll maybe need it walking home," she pondered.

"But the car will bring you back."

"Oh, that will be lovely," she said, and laughed nervously, looking very plain. "Do you know, I know the way we're coming together is terrible, but I can't think of a meeting with Chris as anything but a kind of treat. I've got a sort of party feeling now."

As she held the gate open for me she looked back at the

house.

"It's a horrid little house, isn't it?" she asked. She evidently desired sanction for a long-suppressed discontent.

"It isn't very nice," I agreed.

"They put cows sometimes into the field at the back," she went on, as if conscientiously counting her blessings. "I like that; but otherwise it isn't much."

"But it's got a very pretty name," I said, laying my hand on the raised metal letters that spelled "Mariposa" across the gate.

"Ah, isn't it!" she exclaimed, with the smile of the inveterate romanticist. "It's Spanish, you know, for butterfly."

Once we were in the automobile, she became a little sullen with shyness, because she felt herself so big and clumsy, her clothes so coarse, against the fine upholstery, the silver vase of Christmas roses, and all the deliberate delicacy of Kitty's car. She was afraid of the chauffeur, as the poor are always afraid of men-servants, and ducked her head when he got out to start the car. To recall her to ease and beauty I told her that though Chris had told me all about their meeting, he knew nothing of their parting, and that I wished very much to hear what had happened.

In a deep, embarrassed voice she began to tell me about Monkey Island. It was strange how both Chris and she spoke of it as though it were not a place, but a magic state which largely explained the actions performed in it. Strange, too, that both of them should describe meticulously the one white hawthorn that stood among the poplars by the ferry-side. I suppose a thing that one has looked at with some one one loves acquires forever after a special significance. She said that her father had gone there when she was fourteen. After Mrs. Arlington had been taken away by a swift and painful death the cheer of his Windsor hostelry had become intolerable to the man; he regarded the whole world as her grave, and the tipsy sergeants in scarlet, the carter crying for a pint of four-half, and even the mares dipping their mild noses to the trough in the courtyard seemed to be defiling it by their happy, simple appetites. So they went to Monkey Island, the utter difference of which was a healing, and settled down happily in its green silence. All the summer was lovely; quiet, kind people, schoolmasters who fished, men who wrote books, married couples who still loved solitude, used to come and stay in the bright little inn. And all the winter was lovely, too; her temperament could see an adventure in taking up the carpets because the Thames was coming into the coffee-room. That was the tale of her life for four years. With her head on one side, and the air of judging this question by the light of experience, she pronounced that she had then been happy.

Then one April afternoon Chris landed at the island, and by the first clean, quick movement of tying up his boat made her his slave. I could imagine that it would be so. He was wonderful when he was young; he possessed in great measure the loveliness of young men, which is like the loveliness of the spry foal or the sapling, but in him it was vexed into a serious and moving beauty by the inhabiting soul. When the sunlight lay on him, disclosing the gold hairs on his brown head, or when he was subject to any other physical pleasure, there was always reserve in his response to it. From his eyes, which, though gray, were somehow dark with speculation, one perceived that he was distracted by participation in some spiritual drama. To see him was to desire intimacy with him, so that one might intervene between this body, which was formed for happiness, and this soul, which cherished so deep a faith in tragedy. Well, she gave Chris ducks' eggs for tea. "No one ever had ducks' eggs like father did. It was his way of feeding them. It didn't pay, of course, but they were good." Before the afternoon was out he had snared them all with the silken net of his fine manners; he had talked to father about his poultry and had walked about the runs and shown an intelligent interest, and then, as on many succeeding days, he had laid his charm at the girl's feet. "But I thought he must be some one royal, and when he kept on coming, I thought it must be for the ducks' eggs." Then her damp, dull skin flushed suddenly to a warm glory, and she began to stammer.

"I know all about that," I said quickly. I was more afraid that I should feel envy or any base passion in the presence of this woman than I have ever been of anything else in my life. "I want to hear how you came to part."

"Oh," she cried, "it was the silliest quarrel! We had known how we felt for just a week. Such a week! Lovely weather we had, and father hadn't noticed anything. I didn't want him to, because I thought father might want the marriage soon and think any delay a slight on me, and I knew we would have to wait. Eh! I can remember saying to myself, 'Perhaps five years,' trying to make it as bad as could be so that if we could marry sooner it would be a lovely surprise." She repeated with soft irony, "Perhaps five years!"

"Well, then, one Thursday afternoon I'd gone on the back-water with Bert Batchard, nephew to Mr. Batchard who keeps the inn at Surly Hall. I was laughing out loud because he did row so funny! He's a town chap, and he was handling those oars for all the world as though they were teaspoons. The old dinghy just sat on the water like a hen on its chicks and didn't move, and he so sure of himself! I just sat and laughed and laughed. Then all of a sudden, *clang! clang!* the bell at the ferry. And there was Chris, standing up there among the poplars, his brows straight and black, and not a smile on him. I felt very bad. We picked him up in the dinghy and took him across, and still he didn't smile. He and I got on the island, and Bert, who saw there was something wrong, said, 'Well, I'll toddle off.' And there I was on the lawn with Chris, and he angry and somehow miles away. I remember him saying, 'Here am I coming to say good-by, because I must go away to-night, and I find you larking with that bounder.' And I said: 'O Chris, I've known Bert all my life through him coming to his uncle for the holidays, and we weren't larking. It was only that he couldn't row.' And he went on talking, and then it struck me he wasn't trusting me as he would trust a girl of his own class, and I told him so, and he went on being cruel. Oh, don't make me remember the things we said to each other! It doesn't help. At last I said something awful, and he said: 'Very well; I agree. I'll go,' and he walked over to the boy, who was chopping wood, and got him to take him over in the punt. As he passed me he turned away his face. Well, that's all."

I had got the key at last. There had been a spring at Baldry Court fifteen years ago that was desolate for all that there was beautiful weather. Chris had lingered with Uncle Ambrose in his Thames-side rectory as he had never lingered before, and old Mr. Baldry was filling the house with a sense of hot, apoplectic misery. All day he was up in town at the office, and without explanation he had discontinued his noontide habit of ringing up his wife. All night he used to sit in the library looking over his papers and ledgers; often in the mornings the housemaids would find him asleep across his desk, very red, yet looking dead. The men he

53

brought home to dinner treated him with a kindness and consideration which were not the tributes that that victorious and trumpeting personality was accustomed to exact, and in the course of conversation with them he dropped braggart hints of impending ruin which he would have found it humiliating to address to us directly. At last there came a morning when he said to Mrs. Baldry across the breakfast-table: "I've sent for Chris. If the boy's worth his salt—" It was an appalling admission, like the groan of an old ship as her timbers shiver, from a man who doubted the capacity of his son, as fathers always doubt the capacity of the children born of their old age.

It was that evening, as I went down to see the new baby at the lodge, that I met Chris coming up the drive. Through the blue twilight his white face had had a drowned look. I remembered it well, because my surprise that he passed me without seeing me had made me perceive for the first time that he had never seen me at all save in the most cursory fashion. On the eye of his mind, I realized thenceforward, I had hardly impinged. That night he talked till late with his father, and in the morning he had started for Mexico to keep the mines going, to keep the firm's head above water and Baldry Court sleek and hospitable—to keep everything bright and splendid save only his youth, which ever after that was dulled by care.

Something of this I told Margaret, to which she answered, "Oh, I know all that," and went on with her story. On Sunday, three days after their quarrel, Mr. Allington was found dead in his bed. "I wanted Chris so badly; but he never came, he never wrote," and she fell into a lethargic disposition to sit all day and watch the Thames flow by, from which she was hardly roused by finding that her father had left her nothing save an income of twenty pounds a year from unrealizable stock. She negotiated the transfer of the lease of the inn to a publican, and, after exacting a promise from the new hostess that she would forward all letters that might come, embarked upon an increasingly unfortunate career as a mother's help. First she fell into the hands of a noble Irish family in reduced circumstances, whose conduct in running away and leaving her in a Brighton hotel with her wages and her bill unpaid still distressed and perplexed her. "Why did they do it?" she asked. "I liked them so. The baby was a darling, and Mrs. Murphy had such a nice way of speaking. But it almost makes one think evil of people when they do a thing like that." After two years of less sensational, but still uneasy, adventures, she had come upon a large and needy family called Watson who lived at Chiswick, and almost immediately Mr. William Grey, who was Mrs. Watson's brother, had begun a courtship that I suspected of consisting of an incessant whining up at her protective instinct. "Mr. Grey," she said softly, as though stating his chief aim to affection, "has never been very successful." And still no letter ever came.

So, five years after she left Monkey Island, she married Mr. William Grey. Soon after their marriage he lost his job and was for some time out of work; later he developed a weak chest that needed constant attention. "But it all helped to pass the time," she said cheerfully and without irony. So it happened that it was not till two years after that she had the chance of revisiting Monkey Island. At first there was no money, and later there was the necessity of seeking the healthful breezes of Brighton or Bognor or Southend, which were the places in which Mr. Grey's chest oddly elected to thrive. And when these obstacles were removed, she was lethargic; also she had heard that the inn was not being managed as it ought to be, and she could not have borne to see the green home of her youth defiled. But then there had come a time when she had been very much upset,—she glared a little wildly at me as she said this, as if she would faint if I asked her any questions,—and then she had suddenly become obsessed with a desire to see Monkey Island once more.

"Well, when we got to the ferry, Mr. Grey says, 'But mercy, Margaret, there's water all round it!' and I said, 'William, that's just it.'" They found that the island was clean and decorous again, for it had only recently changed hands. "Father and daughter the new people are, just like me and dad, and Mr. Taylor's something of dad's cut, too, but he comes from the North. But Miss Taylor's much handsomer than I ever was; a really big woman she is, and such lovely golden hair. They were very kind when I told them who I was; gave us duck and green peas for lunch and I did think of dad. They were nothing like as good as his ducks, but then I expect they paid. And then Miss Taylor took William out to look at the garden. I knew he didn't like it, for he's always shy with a showy woman, and I was going after them when Mr. Taylor said: 'Here, stop a minute. I've got something here that may interest you. Just come in here. He took me up to the roller desk in the office, and out of the drawer he took twelve letters addressed to me in Chris's handwriting.

"He was a kind man. He put me into a chair and called Miss Taylor in and told her to keep William out in the garden as long as possible. At last I said, 'But Mrs. Hitchcock did say she'd send my letters on.' And he said, 'Mrs. Hitchcock hadn't been here three weeks before she bolted with a bookie from Bray, and after that Hitchcock mixed his drinks and got careless.' He said they had found these stuffed into the desk."

"And what was in them?"

"For a long time I did not read them; I thought it was against my duty as a wife. But when I got that telegram saying he was wounded, I went up-stairs and read those letters. Oh, those letters!"

She bowed her head and wept.

As the car swung through the gates of Baldry Court she sat up and dried her eyes. She looked out at the strip of turf, so bright that one would think it wet, and lighted here and there with snowdrops and scillas and crocuses, that runs between the drive and the tangle of silver birch and bramble and fern. There is no esthetic reason for that border; the common outside looks lovelier where it fringes the road with dark gorse and rough amber grasses. Its use is purely philosophic; it proclaims that here we esteem only controlled beauty, that the wild will not have its way within our gates, that it must be made delicate and decorated into felicity. Surely, she must see that this was no place for beauty that had been not mellowed, but lacerated, by time, that no one accustomed to live here could help wincing at such external dinginess as hers. But instead she said: "It's a big place. Chris must have worked hard to keep all this up." The pity of this woman was like a flaming sword. No one had ever before pitied Chris for the magnificence of Baldry Court. It had been our pretense that by wearing costly clothes and organizing a costly life we had been the servants of his desire. But she revealed the truth that, although he did indeed desire a magnificent house, it was a house not built with hands.

But that she was wise, that the angels would of a certainty be on her side, did not make her any the less physically offensive to our atmosphere. All my doubts as to the wisdom of my expedition revived in the little time we had to spend in the hall waiting for the tea which I had ordered in the hope that it might help Margaret to compose her distressed face. She hovered with her back to the oak table, fumbling with her thread gloves, winking her tear-red eyes, tapping with her foot on the carpet, throwing her weight from one leg to the other, and I constantly contrasted her appearance by some clumsiness with the new acquisition of Kitty's decorative genius that stood so close behind her on the table that I was afraid it might be upset by one of her spasmodic movements. This was a shallow black bowl in the center of which crouched on all fours a white, naked nymph, her small head intently drooped to the white flowers that floated on the black waters all around her. Beside the pure black of the bowl her rusty plumes looked horrible; beside that white nymph, eternally innocent of all but the contemplation of beauty, her opaque skin and her suffering were offensive; beside its air of being the coolly conceived and leisurely executed production of a hand and brain lifted by their rare quality to the service of the not absolutely necessary, her appearance of having only for the moment ceased to cope with a vexed and needy environment struck me as a cancerous blot on the fair world. Perhaps it was absurd to pay attention to this indictment of a noble woman by a potter's toy, but that toy happened to be also a little image of Chris's conception of women. Exquisite we were according to our equipment, unflushed by appetite or passion, even noble passion, our small heads bent intently on the white flowers of luxury floating on the black waters of life, he had known none other than us. With such a mental habit a man could not help but wince at Margaret. I drank my tea very slowly because I previsioned what must happen in the next five minutes. Down there by the pond he would turn at the sound of those heavy boots on the path, and with one glance he would assess the age of her, the rubbed surface of her, the torn fine texture, and he would show to her squalid mask just such a blank face as he had shown to Kitty's piteous mask the night before. Although I had a gift for self-pity, I knew her case would then be worse than mine; for it would be worse to see, as she would see, the ardor in his eyes give place to kindliness than never to have ardor there. He would hesitate; she would make one of her harassed gestures, and trail away with that wet, patient look which was her special line. He would go back to his boyish sport with the skiff; I hoped the brown waters would not seem too kind. She would go back to Mariposa, sit on her bed, and read those letters.

"And now," she said brightly as I put down my cup, "may I see Chris?" She had not a doubt of the enterprise.

I took her into the drawing-room and opened one of the French windows.

"Go past the cedars to the pond," I told her. "He is rowing there."

"That is nice," she said. "He always looks so lovely in a boat."

I called after her, trying to hint the possibility of a panic breakdown to their meeting:

"You'll find he's altered—"

She cried gleefully:

"Oh, I shall know him."

As I went up-stairs I became aware that I was near to a bodily collapse; I suppose the truth is that I was physically so jealous of Margaret that it was making me ill. But suddenly, like a tired person dropping a weight that they know to be precious, but cannot carry for another minute, my mind refused to consider the situation any longer and turned to the perception of material things. I leaned over the balustrade and looked down at the fineness of the hall: the deliberate figure of the nymph in her circle of black waters, the clear pink-and-white of Kitty's chintz, the limpid surface of the oak, the broken burning of all the gay reflected colors in the paneled walls. I said to myself, "If everything else goes, there is always this to fall back on," and I went on, pleased that I was wearing delicate stuffs and that I had a smooth skin, pleased that the walls of the corridor were so soft a twilight blue, pleased that through a far-off open door there came a stream of light that made the carpet blaze its stronger blue. And when I saw that it was the nursery door that was open, and that Kitty was sitting in Nanny's big chair by the window, I did not care about the peaked face she lifted, its fairness palely gilt by the March sunlight, or the tremendous implications of the fact that she had come to her dead child's nursery although she had not washed her hair. I said sternly, because she had forgotten that we lived in the impregnable fort of a gracious life:

"O Kitty, that poor battered thing outside!"

She stared so grimly out into the garden that my eyes followed her stare.

It was one of those draggled days, common at the end of March when a garden looks at its worst. The wind that was rolling up to check a show of sunshine had taken away the cedar's dignity of solid blue shade, had set the black firs beating their arms together, and had filled the sky with glaring gray clouds that dimmed the brilliance of the crocuses. It was to give gardens a point on days such as these, when the planned climax of this flower-bed and that stately tree goes for nothing, that the old gardeners raised statues in their lawns and walks, large things with a subject, mossy Tritons or nymphs with an urn, that held the eye. Even so in this unrestful garden one's eyes lay on the figure in the yellow raincoat that was standing still in the middle of the lawn.

How her near presence had been known by Chris I do not understand, but there he was, running across the lawn as night after night I had seen him in my dreams running across No-Man's-Land. I knew that so he would close his eyes as he ran; I knew that so he would pitch on his knees when he reached safety. I assumed naturally that at Margaret's feet lay safety even before I saw her arms brace him under the armpits with a gesture that was not passionate, but rather the movement of one carrying a wounded man from under fire. But even when she had raised his head to the level of her lips, the central issue was not decided. I covered my eyes and said aloud, "In a minute he will see her face, her hands." But although it was a long time before I looked again, they were still clinging breast to breast. It was as though her embrace fed him, he looked so strong as he broke away. They stood with clasped hands looking at one another. They looked straight, they looked delightedly! And then, as if resuming a conversation tiresomely interrupted by some social obligation, they drew together again, and passed under the tossing branches of the cedar to the wood beyond. I reflected, while Kitty shrilly wept, how entirely right Chris had been in his assertion that to lovers innumerable things do not matter.

CHAPTER 5

AFTER the automobile had taken Margaret away Chris came to us as we sat in the drawing-room, and, after standing for a while in the glow of the fire, hesitantly said:

"I want to tell you that I know it is all right. Margaret has explained to me."

Kitty crumpled her sewing into a white ball.

"You mean, I suppose, that you know I'm your wife. I'm pleased that you describe that as knowing 'it's all right,' and grateful that you have accepted it at last—on Margaret's authority. This is an occasion that would make any wife proud."

Her irony was as faintly acrid as a caraway-seed, and never afterward did she reach even that low pitch of violence; for from that mild, forward droop of the head with which he received the mental lunge she realized suddenly that this was no pretense and that something as impassable as death lay between them. Thereafter his proceedings evoked no comment but suffering. There was nothing to say when all day, save for those hours of the afternoon that Margaret spent with him, he sat like a blind man waiting for his darkness to lift. There was nothing to say when he did not seem to see our flowers, yet kept till they rotted the daffodils which Margaret brought from the garden that looked like an allotment.

So Kitty lay about like a broken doll, face downward

on a sofa, with one limp arm dangling to the floor, or protruding stiff feet in fantastic slippers from the end of her curtained bed; and I tried to make my permanent wear that mood which had mitigated the end of my journey with Margaret—a mood of intense perception in which my strained mind settled on every vivid object that came under my eyes and tried to identify myself with its brightness and its lack of human passion. This does not mean that I passed my day in a state of joyous appreciation; it means that many times in the lanes of Harrowweald I have stood for long looking up at a fine tracery of bare boughs against the hard, high spring sky while the cold wind rushed through my skirts and chilled me to the bone, because I was afraid that when I moved my body and my attention I might begin to think. Indeed, grief is not the clear melancholy the young believe it. It is like a siege in a tropical city. The skin dries and the throat parches as though one were living in the heat of the desert; water and wine taste warm in the mouth, and food is of the substance of the sand; one snarls at one's company; thoughts prick one through sleep like mosquitos.

A week after my journey to Wealdstone I went to Kitty to ask her to come for a walk with me and found her stretched on her pillows, holding a review of her under-clothing. She refused bitterly and added:

"Be back early. Remember Dr. Gilbert Anderson is coming at half-past four. He's our last hope. And tell that woman she must see him. He says he wants to see every-body concerned." She continued to look wanly at the frail, luminous silks her maid brought her as a speculator who had cornered an article for which there had been no de-mand might look at his damnably numerous, damnably unprofitable freights. So I went out alone into a soft day, with the dispelled winter lurking above in high dark clouds, under which there ran quick, fresh currents of air and broken shafts of insistent sunshine that spread a gray clarity of light in which every color showed sharp and strong. On the breast that Harrowweald turns to the south they had set a lambing-yard. The pale-lavender hurdles and gold-strewn straw were new gay notes on the opaque winter green of the slope, and the apprehensive bleatings of the ewes wound about the hill like a river of sound as they were driven up a lane hidden by the hedge. The lines of bare elms darkening the plains below made it seem as though the tide of winter had fallen and left this bare and sparkling in the spring. I liked it so much that I opened the gate and went and sat down on a tree which had been torn up by the roots in the great gale last year, but had not yet resigned itself to death, and was bravely decking its boughs with purple elm-flowers.

That pleased me, too, and I wished I had some one with me to enjoy this artless little show of the new year. I had not really wanted Kitty; the companions I needed were Chris and Margaret. Chris would have talked, as he loved to do when he looked at leisure on a broad valley, about ideas which he had to exclude from his ordinary hours lest they should break the power of business over his mind, and Margaret would have gravely watched the argument from the shadow of her broad hat to see that it kept true, like a housewife watching a saucepan of milk lest it should boil over. They were naturally my friends, these gentle, speculative people.

Then suddenly I was stunned with jealousy. It was not their love for each other that caused me such agony at that moment; it was the thought of the things their eyes had rested upon together. I imagined that white hawthorn among the poplars by the ferry on which they had looked fifteen years ago at Monkey Island, and it was more than I could bear. I thought how even now they might be exclaiming at the green smoke of the first buds on the brown undergrowth by the pond, and at that I slid off the tree-trunk and began walking very quickly down the hill. The red cows drank from the pond cupped by the willow-roots; a raw-boned stallion danced clumsily because warmth was running through the ground. I found a stream in the fields and followed it till it became a shining dike embanked with glowing green and gold mosses in the midst of woods; and the sight of those things was no sort of joy, because my vision was solitary. I wanted to end my desperation by leaping from a height, and I climbed on a knoll and flung myself face downward on the dead leaves below.

I was now utterly cut off from Chris. Before, when I looked at him, I knew an instant ease in the sight of the short golden down on his cheeks, the ridge of bronze flesh above his thick, fair eyebrows. But now I was too busy reassuring him by showing a steady, undistorted profile crowned by a neat, proud sweep of hair instead of the tear-darkened mask he always feared ever to have enough vitality left over to enjoy his presence. I spoke in a calm voice full from the chest, quite unfluted with agony; I read "Country Life" with ponderous interest; I kept my hands, which I desired to wring, in doeskin gloves for most of the day; I played with the dogs a great deal and wore my thickest tweeds; I pretended that the slight heaviness of my features is a correct indication of my temperament. The only occasion when I could safely let the sense of him saturate me as it used was when I met Margaret in the hall as she came or went. She was very different now; she had a little smile in her eyes, as though she were listening to a familiar air played far away. Her awkwardness seemed indecision as to whether she should walk or dance to that distant music; her shabbiness was no more repulsive than the untidiness of a child who had been so eager to get to the party that it has not let its nurse finish fastening its frock. Always she extended a hand in an unbuttoned black thread glove and said, "It's another fine day again," or diffidently, as Kitty continued to withhold her presence, "I hope Mrs. Baldry is keeping well." Then, as our hands touched, he was with us, invoked by our common adoration. I felt his rough male texture and saw the clear warmth of his brown and gold coloring; I thought of him with the passion of exile. To Margaret it was a call, and she moved past me to the garden, holding her hands in front of her as though she bore invisible gifts, and pausing on the step of the French window to smile to herself, as if in her heart she turned over the precious thought: "He is here. This garden holds him." My moment, my small sole subsistence, ended in a feeling of jealousy as ugly and unmental as sickness. This was the saddest spring.

Nothing could mitigate the harshness of our dejection. You may think we were attaching an altogether fictitious importance to what was merely the delusion of a madman. But every minute of the day, particularly at those trying times when he strolled about the house and grounds with the doctors, smiling courteously, but without joy, and answering their questions with the crisp politeness of a man shaking off an inquisitive commercial traveler in a hotel smoking-room, it became plain that if madness means a liability to wild error about the world Chris was not mad. It was our peculiar shame that he had rejected us when he had attained to something saner than sanity. His very loss of memory was a triumph over the limitations of language which prevent the mass of men from making explicit statements about their spiritual relationships. If he had said to Kitty and me, "I do not know you," we would have gaped; if he had expanded his meaning and said, "You are nothing to me; my heart is separate from your hearts," we would have wept at an unkindness he had not intended. But by the blankness of those eyes which saw me only as a disregarded playmate and Kitty not at all save as a stranger who had somehow become a decorative presence in his home and the orderer of his meals he let us know completely where we were. Even though I lay weeping at it on the dead leaves I was sensible of the bitter rapture which attends the discovery of any truth. I felt, indeed, a cold intellectual pride in his refusal to remember his prosperous maturity and his determined dwelling in the time of his first love, for it showed him so much saner than the rest of us, who take life as it comes, loaded with the unessential and the irritating. I was even willing to admit that this choice of what was to him reality out of all the appearances so copiously presented by the world, this adroit recovery of the dropped pearl of beauty, was the act of genius I had always expected from him. But that did not make less agonizing this exclusion from his life.

I could not think clearly about it. I suppose that the subject of our tragedy, written in spiritual terms, was that in Kitty he had turned from the type of woman that makes the body conqueror of the soul and in me the type that mediates between the soul and the body and makes them run even and unhasty like a well-matched pair of carriage horses, and had given himself to a woman whose bleak habit it was to champion the soul against the body. But I saw it just as a fantastic act of cruelty that I could think of only as a conjunction of calamitous images. I think

of it happening somewhere behind the front, at the end
of a straight road that runs by a line of ragged poplars
between mud flats made steel-bright with floods pitted
by the soft, slow rain. There, past a church that lacks its
tower, stand a score of houses, each hideous with patches
of bare bricks that show like sores through the ripped-off
plaster and uncovered rafters that stick out like broken
bones. There are people still living here. A slouchy woman
sits at the door of a filthy cottage, counting some dirty
linen and waving her bare arm at some passing soldiers.
And at another house there is a general store with strings
of orange onions and bunches of herbs hanging from the
roof, a brown gloom rich with garlic and humming with
the flies that live all the year round in French village shops,
a black cat rubbing her sleepiness against the lintel. It is in
there that Chris is standing, facing across the counter an
old man in a blouse, with a scar running white into the gray
thickets of his beard, an old man with a smile at once lewd
and benevolent, repulsive with dirt and yet magnificent by
reason of the Olympian structure of his body. I think he is
the soul of the universe, equally cognizant and disregardful
of every living thing, to whom I am not more dear than the
bare-armed slouchy woman at the neighboring door. And
Chris is leaning on the counter, his eyes glazed. (This is his
spirit; his body lies out there in the drizzle, at the other end
of the road.) He is looking down on the two crystal balls
that the old man's foul, strong hands have rolled across
to him. In one he sees Margaret, not in her raincoat and
her nodding plumes, but as she is transfigured in the light
of eternity. Long he looks there; then drops a glance to
the other, just long enough to see that in its depths Kitty
and I walk in bright dresses through our glowing gardens.
We had suffered no transfiguration, for we are as we are,

and there is nothing more to us. The whole truth about us lies in our material seeming. He sighs a deep sigh of delight and puts out his hand to the ball where Margaret shines. His sleeve catches the other one and sends it down to crash in a thousand pieces on the floor. The old man's smile continues to be lewd and benevolent; he is still not more interested in me than in the bare-armed woman. Chris is wholly inclosed in his intentness on his chosen crystal. No one weeps for this shattering of our world.

I stirred on the dead leaves as though I had really heard the breaking of the globe and cried out, "Gilbert Anderson, Gilbert Anderson must cure him." Heaven knows that I had no reason for faith in any doctor, for during the last week so many of them, as sleek as seals with their neatly brushed hair and their frock-coats, had stood round Chris and looked at him with the consequenceless deliberation of a plumber. Their most successful enterprise had been his futile hypnotism. He had submitted to it as a good-natured man submits to being blindfolded at a children's party, and under its influence had recovered his memory and his middle-aged personality, had talked of Kitty with the humorous tenderness of the English husband, and had looked possessively about him. But as his mind came out of the control he exposed their lie that they were dealing with a mere breakdown of the normal process by pushing away this knowledge and turning to them the blank wall, all the blanker because it was unconscious, of his resolution not to know. I had accepted that it would always be so. But at that moment I had so great a need to throw off my mood of despair, so insupportably loaded with all the fantastic images to which my fevered mind transmuted the facts of our tragedy, that I filled myself with a gasping, urgent faith in this new doctor. I jumped up and pushed through the brambles to the hedge that divided the preserves in which I was trespassing from our own woods, breathless because I had let it go past four and I had still to find Chris and Margaret for the doctor's visit at the half-hour.

There had been a hardening of the light while I slept that made the dear, familiar woods rich and sinister, and to the eye, tropical. The jewel-bright buds on the soot-black boughs, the blue valley distances, smudged here and there with the pink enamel of villa-roofs, and seen between the black-and-white intricacies of the birch-trunks and the luminous gray pillars of the beeches, hurt my wet eyes as might beauty blazing under an equatorial sun. There was a tropical sense of danger, too, for I walked as apprehensively as though a snake coiled under every leaf, because I feared to come on them when he was speaking to her without looking at her or thinking in silence while he played with her hand. Embraces do not matter; they merely indicate the will to love, and may as well be followed by defeat as victory. But disregard means that now there needs to be no straining of the eyes, no stretching forth of the hands, no pressing of the lips, because theirs is such a union that they are no longer aware of the division of their flesh. I know it must be so; a lonely life gives one opportunities of thinking these things out. I could not have borne to see signs of how he had achieved this intimacy with the woman whom a sudden widening of the downward vista showed as she leaned her bent back, ridged by her cheap stays, against a birch that some special skill of our forester had made wonderful for its straight slenderness. Against the clear colors of the bright bare wood her yellow raincoat made a muddy patch, and as a dead bough dropped near her she made a squalid dodging movement like a hen. She was not so much a person as an implication of dreary poverty, like an open door in a mean house that lets out the smell of cook-ing cabbage and the screams of children. Doubtlessly he sat somewhere close to her, lumpishly content. I thought distractedly how necessary it was that Gilbert Anderson should cure him, and tried to shout to her, but found my throat full of sobs. So I broke my way down through the fern and bramble and stood level with them, though still divided by some yards of broken ground.

It was not utter dullness not to have anticipated the beauty that I saw. No one could have told. They had taken the mackintosh rug out of the dinghy and spread it on this little space of clear grass, I think so that they could look at a scattering of early primroses in a pool of white anemones at an oak-tree's foot. She had run her hands over the rug so that it lay quite smooth and comfortable under him when at last he felt drowsy and turned on his side to sleep. He lay there in the confiding relaxation of a sleeping child, his hands unclenched, and his head thrown back so that the bare throat showed defenselessly. Now he was asleep and his face undarkened by thought, one saw how very fair he really was. And she, her mournfully vigilant face pinkened by the cold river of air sent by the advancing evening through the screen of rusted-gold bracken behind her, was sitting by him, just watching.

I have often seen people grouped like that on the com-mon outside our gates on Bank holidays. Most often the man has a handkerchief over his face to shade him from the sun, and the woman squats beside him and peers through the undergrowth to see that the children come to no harm as they play. It has sometimes seemed to me that there was a significance about it. You know when one goes into the damp, odorous coolness of a church in a Catholic country and sees the kneeling worshipers, their bodies bent stiffly and reluctantly, and yet with abandonment as though to represent the inevitable bending of the will to a purpose outside the individual person, or when under any sky one sees a mother with her child in her arms, something turns in one's heart like a sword, and one says to oneself, "If humanity forgets these attitudes there is an end to the world." But people like me, who are not artists, are never sure about people they don't know. So it was not until now, when it happened to my friends, when it was my dear Chris and my dear Margaret who sat thus englobed in peace as in a crystal sphere, that I knew it was the most significant, as it was the loveliest, attitude in the world. It means that the woman has gathered the soul of the man into her soul and is keeping it warm in love and peace so that his body can rest quiet for a little time. That is a great thing for a woman to do. I know there are things at least as great for those women whose independent spirits can ride fearlessly and with interest outside the home park of their personal relationships, but independence is not the occupation of most of us. What we desire is greatness such as this, which had given sleep to the beloved. I had known that he was having bad nights at Baldry Court in that new room with the jade-green painted walls and the lapis-lazuli fireplace, which he found with surprise to be his instead of the remembered little room with the fishing-rods; but I had not been able to do anything about it.

It was not fair that by the exercise of a generosity which seemed as fortuitous a possession as a beautiful voice a woman should be able to do such wonderful things for a man. For sleep was the least of her gifts to him. What she had done in leading him into the quiet magic circle out of our life, out of the splendid house which was not so much a house as a vast piece of space partitioned off from the universe and decorated partly for beauty and partly to make our privacy more insolent, out of the garden where the flowers took thought as to how they should grow and the wood made as formal as a pillared aisle by forestry, may be judged from my anguish in being left there alone. Indeed she had been generous to us all, for at her touch our lives had at last fallen into a pattern; she was the sober thread the interweaving of which with our scattered magnificences had somewhat achieved the design that otherwise would not appear. Perhaps even her dinginess was part of her generosity, for in order to fit into the pattern one has sometimes to forego something of one's individual beauty. That is why women like us do not wear such obviously lovely dresses as cocottes, but clothe ourselves in garments that by their slight neglect of the possibilities of beauty declare that there are such things as thrift and restraint and care for the future. And so I could believe of Margaret that her determined dwelling in places where there was not enough of anything, her continued exposure of herself to the grime of squalid living, was unconsciously deliberate. The deep internal thing that had guided Chris to forgetfulness had guided her to poverty, so that when the time came for her meeting with her lover there should be not one intimation of the beauty of suave flesh to distract him from the message of her soul. I looked upward at this supreme act of sacrifice and glowed at her private gift to me. My sleep, though short, was now dreamless. No more did I see his body rotting into union with that brown texture of corruption which is No-Man's-Land; no more did I see him slipping softly down the parapet into the trench; no more did I hear voices talking in a void: "Help me, old man; I've got no legs—" "I can't, old man; I've got no hands." They could not take him back to the army as he was. Only that morning as I went through the library he had raised an appalled face from the pages of a history of the war.

"Jenny, it can't be true that they did that to Belgium? Those funny, quiet, stingy people!" And his soldierly knowledge was as deeply buried as this memory of that awful August. While her spell endured they could not send him back into the hell of war. This wonderful, kind woman held his body as safely as she held his soul.

I was so grateful that I was forced to go and sit down on the rug beside her. It was an intrusion, but I wanted to be near her. She did not look surprised when she turned to me her puckered brows, but smiled through the ugly fringe of vagrant hairs the weather had plucked from under the hard rim of her hat. It was part of her loveliness that even if she did not understand an act she could accept it.

Presently she leaned over to me across his body and whispered:

"He's not cold. I put the overcoat on him as soon as he was fairly off. I've just felt his hands, and they're as warm as toast." If I had whispered like that I would have wakened him.

Soon he stirred, groped for her hand, and lay with his cheek against the rough palm. He was awake, but liked to lie so.

In a little she shook her hand away and said:

"Get up and run along to the house and have some hot tea. You'll catch your death lying out here."

He caught her hand again. It was evident that for some reason the moment was charged with ecstasy for them both.

It seemed as though there was a softer air in this small clearing than anywhere else in the world. I stood up, with my back against a birch and said negligently, knowing now that nothing could really threaten them:

"There is a doctor coming at half-past four who wants to see you both."

It cast no shadow on their serenity. He smiled upward, still lying on his back, and hailed me, "Hallo, Jenny." But she made him get up and help her to fold the rug.

"It's not right to keep a doctor waiting in these times," she declared, "so overworked they are, poor men, since the war." As I led the way up through the woods to the house I heard her prove her point by an illustrative anecdote about something that had happened down her road. I heard, too, their footsteps come to a halt for a space. I think her gray eyes had looked at him so sweetly that he had been constrained to take her in his arms.

CHAPTER 6

I FELT, I remember with the little perk of self-approbation with which one remembers any sort of accurate premonition even if its fulfilment means disaster, a cold hand close round my heart as we turned the corner of the house and came on Dr. Gilbert Anderson. I was startled, to begin with, by his unmedical appearance. He was a little man with winking blue eyes, a flushed and crumpled forehead, a little gray mustache that gave him the profile of an amiable cat, and a lively taste in spotted ties, and he lacked that appetiteless look which is affected by distinguished practitioners. He was at once more comical and more suggestive of power than any other doctor I had ever seen, and this difference was emphasized by his unexpected occupation. A tennis-ball which he had discovered somewhere had roused his sporting instincts, and he was trying at what range it was possible to kick it between two large stones which he had placed close together in front of the steps up to the house. It was his chubby absorption in this amusement which accounted for his first moment of embarrassment.

"Nobody about in there; we professional men get so little fresh air," he said bluffly, and blew his nose in a very large handkerchief, from the folds of which he emerged with perfect self-possession. "You," he said to Chris, with a naïve adoption of the detective tone, "are the patient." He rolled his blue eye on me, took a good look, and, as he realized I did not matter, shook off the unnecessary impression like a dog coming out of water. He faced Margaret as though she were the nurse in charge of the case and gave her a brisk little nod. "You're Mrs. Grey. I shall want to talk to you later. Meantime—this man. I'll come back." He indicated by a windmill gesture that we should go into the house, and swung off with Chris.

She obeyed; that sort of woman always does what the doctor orders. But I delayed for a moment to stare after this singular specialist, to sidetrack my foreboding by pronouncing him a bounder, to wish, as my foreboding persisted, that like a servant I could give notice because there was "always something happening in the house."

Then, as the obedient figure at the top of the stairs was plainly shivering under its shoddy clothes in the rising wind that was polishing the end of the afternoon to brightness, I hastened to lead her into the hall. We stood about uneasily in its gloaming. Margaret looked round her and said in a voice flattened by the despondency she evidently shared with me: "It is nice to have everything ready that people can want and everything in its place. I used to do it at Monkey Island Inn. It was not grand like this, of course, but our visitors always came back a second time." Abstractedly and yet with joy she fingered the fine work of the table-leg.

There was a noise above us like the fluttering of doves. Kitty was coming downstairs in a white serge dress against which her hands were rosy; a woman with such lovely little hands never needed to wear flowers. By her kind of physical discipline she had reduced her grief to no more than a slight darkening under the eyes, and for this moment she was glowing. I knew it was because she was going to meet a new man and anticipated the kindling of admiration in his eyes, and I smiled, contrasting her probable prefiguring of Dr. Anderson with the amiable rotundity we had just encountered. Not that it would have made any difference if she had seen him. Beautiful women of her type lose, in this matter of admiration alone, their otherwise tremendous sense of class distinction; they are obscurely aware that it is their civilizing mission to flash the jewel of their beauty before all men, so that they shall desire it and work to get the wealth to buy it, and thus be seduced by a present appetite to a tilling of the earth that serves the future. There is, you know, really room for all of us; we each have our peculiar use.

"The doctor's talking to Chris outside," I said.

"Ah," breathed Kitty. I found, though the occasion was a little grim, some entertainment in the two women's faces, so mutually intent, so differently fair, the one a polished surface that reflected light, like a mirror hung opposite a window, the other a lamp grimed by the smoke of careless use, but still giving out radiance from its burning oil. Margaret was smiling wonderingly up at this prettiness, but Kitty seemed to be doing some brainwork.

"How do you do, Mrs. Grey?" she said, suddenly shaking out her cordiality as one shakes out a fan. "It's very kind of you. Won't you go up-stairs and take off your things?"

"No, thank you," answered Margaret, shyly, "I shall have to go away so soon."

"Ah, do!" begged Kitty, prettily.

It was, of course, that she did not want Margaret to meet the specialist in those awful clothes; but I did not darken the situation by explaining that this disaster had already happened. Instead, I turned to Margaret an expression which conveyed that this was an act of hospitality the refusal of which we would find wounding, and to that she yielded, as I knew she would. She followed me up-stairs and along the corridors very slowly, like a child paddling in a summer sea. She enjoyed the feeling of the thick carpet underfoot; she looked lingeringly at the pictures on the wall; occasionally she put a finger to touch a vase as if by that she made its preciousness more her own. Her spirit, I could see, was as deeply concerned about Chris as was mine; but she had such faith in life that she retained serenity enough to enjoy what beauty she came across in her period of waiting. Even her enjoyment was indirectly generous. When she came into my room the backward flinging of her head and her deep "Oh!" recalled to me what I had long forgotten, how fine were its proportions, how clever the grooved arch above the window, how like the evening sky my blue curtains.

"And the lovely things you have on your dressing-table," she commented. "You must have very good taste." The charity that changed my riches to a merit! As I helped her to take off her raincoat and reflected that Kitty would not be pleased when she saw that the removal of the garment disclosed a purple blouse of stuff called moirette that servants use for petticoats, she exclaimed softly Kitty's praises. "I know I shouldn't make personal remarks, but Mrs. Baldry is lovely. She has three circles round her neck. I've only two." It was a touching betrayal that she possessed that intimate knowledge of her own person which comes to women who have been loved. I could not for the life of me have told you how many circles there were round my neck. Plainly discontented with herself in the midst of all this fineness, she said diffidently, "Please, I would like to do my hair." So I pulled the arm-chair up to the dressing-table, and leaned on its back while she, sitting shyly on its very edge, unpinned her two long braids, so thick, so dull.

"You've lovely hair," I said.

"I used to have nice hair," she mourned, "but these last few years I've let myself go." She made half-hearted attempts to smooth the straggling tendrils on her temples, but presently laid down her brush and clicked her tongue against her teeth. "I hope that man's not worrying Chris," she said.

There was no reassurance ready, so I went to the other side of the room to put her hat down on a chair, and stayed for a moment to pat its plumes and wonder if nothing could be done with it. But it was, as surgeons say, an inoperable case. So I just gloomed at it and wished I had not let this doctor interpose his plumpness between Chris and Margaret, who since that afternoon seemed to me as not only a woman whom it was good to love, but, as a patron saint must appear to a Catholic, as an intercessory being whose kindliness could be daunted only by some special and incredibly malicious decision of the Supreme Force. I was standing with eyes closed and my hands abstractedly stroking the hat that was the emblem of her martyrdom, and I was thinking of her in a way that was a prayer to her, when I heard her sharp cry. That she, whose essence was a patient silence, should cry out sharply, startled me strangely. I turned quickly.

She was standing up, and in her hand she held the photograph of Oliver that I keep on my dressing-table. It is his last photograph, the one taken just a week before he died.

"Who is this?" she asked.

"The only child Chris ever had. He died five years ago."

"Five years ago?"

Why did it matter so?

"Yes," I said.

"*He* died five years ago, my Dick." Her eyes grew great. "How old was he?"

"Just two."

"My Dick was two." We both were breathing hard. "Why did he die?"

"We never knew. He was the loveliest boy, but delicate from his birth. At the end he just faded away, with the merest cold."

"So did my Dick—a chill. We thought he would be up and about the next day, and he just—"

Her awful gesture of regret was suddenly paralyzed. She seemed to be fighting her way to a discovery.

"It's—it's as if," she stammered, "they each had half a life."

I felt the usual instinct to treat her as though she were ill, because it was evident that she was sustained by a mystic interpretation of life. But she had already taught me something, so I stood aside while she fell on her knees, and wondered why she did not look at the child's photograph, but pressed it to her bosom, as though to stanch a wound. I thought, as I have often thought before, that the childless have the greatest joy in children, for to us they are just slips of immaturity lovelier than the flowers and with the power over the heart, but to mothers they are fleshly cables binding one down to such profundities of feeling as the awful agony that now possessed her. For although I knew I would have accepted it with rapture because it was the result of intimacy with Chris, its awfulness appalled me. Not only did it make my body hurt with sympathy; it shook the ground beneath my feet. For that her serenity, which a moment before had seemed as steady as the earth and as all-enveloping as the sky, should be so utterly dispelled made me aware that I had of late been underestimating the cruelty of the order of things. Lovers are frustrated; children are not begotten that should have had the loveliest life; the pale usurpers of their birth die young. Such a world will not suffer magic circles to endure.

The parlor-maid knocked at the door.

"Mrs. Baldry and Dr. Anderson are waiting in the drawing-room, ma'am."

Margaret reassumed her majesty, and put her white face close to the glass as she pinned up her braids.

"I knew there was a something," she moaned, and set the hair-pins all awry. More she could not say, though I clung to her and begged her; but the slow gesture with which, as we were about to leave the room, she laid her hand across the child's photograph somehow convinced me that we were not to be victorious.

When we went into the drawing-room we found Dr. Anderson, plump and expository, balancing himself on the balls of his feet on the hearth-rug and enjoying the caress of the fire on his calves, while Kitty, showing against the dark frame of her oak chair like a white rosebud that was still too innocent to bloom, listened with that slight reservation of the attention customary in beautiful women.

"A complete case of amnesia," he was saying as Margaret, white-lipped, yet less shy than I had ever seen her, went to a seat by the window, and I sank down on the sofa. "His unconscious self is refusing to let him resume his relations with his normal life, and so we get this loss of memory."

"I've always said," declared Kitty, with an air of good sense, "that if he would make an effort—"

"Effort!" He jerked his round head about. "The mental life that can be controlled by effort isn't the mental life that matters. You've been stuffed up when you were young with talk about a thing called self-control, a sort of barmaid of the soul that says, 'Time's up, gentlemen,' and 'Here, you've had enough.' There's no such thing. There's a deep self in one, the essential self, that has its wishes. And if those wishes are suppressed by the superficial self,—the self that makes, as you say, efforts, and usually makes them with the sole idea of putting up a good show before the neighbors,— it takes its revenge. Into the house of conduct erected by the superficial self it sends an obsession, which doesn't, owing to a twist that the superficial self, which isn't candid, gives it, seem to bear any relation to the suppressed wish. A man who really wants to leave his wife develops a hatred for pickled cabbage which may find vent in performances that lead straight to the asylum. But that's all technical," he finished bluffly. "My business to understand it, not yours. The point is, Mr. Baldry's obsession is that he can't remember the latter years of his life. Well,"—his winking blue eyes drew us all into a community we hardly felt,—"what's the suppressed wish of which it's the manifestation?"

"He wished for nothing," said Kitty. "He was fond of us, and he had a lot of money."

"Ah, but he did!" countered the doctor, gleefully. He seemed to be enjoying it all. "Quite obviously he has forgotten his life here because he is discontented with it. What clearer proof could you need than the fact you were just telling me when these ladies came in—that the reason the War Office didn't wire to you when he was wounded was that he had forgotten to register his address? Don't you see what that means?"

"Forgetfulness," shrugged Kitty. "He isn't businesslike." She had always nourished a doubt as to whether Chris was really, as she put it, practical, and his income and his international reputation weighed nothing as against his evident inability to pick up pieces at sales.

"One forgets only those things that one wants to forget. It's our business to find out why he wanted to forget this life."

"He can remember quite well when he is hypnotized," she said obstructively. She had quite ceased to glow.

"Oh, hypnotism's a silly trick. It releases the memory of a dissociated personality which can't be related—not possibly in such an obstinate case as this—to the waking personality. I'll do it by talking to him. Getting him to tell his dreams." He beamed at the prospect. "But you—it would be such a help if you would give me any clue to this discontent."

"I tell you," said Kitty, "he was not discontented till he went mad."

He caught the glint of her rising temper.

"Ah," he said, "madness is an indictment not of the people one lives with, only of the high gods. If there was anything, it's evident that it was not your fault." A smile sugared it, and knowing that where he had to flatter his dissecting hand had not an easy task, he turned to me, whose general appearance suggests that flattery is not part of my daily diet. "You, Miss Baldry, you've known him longest."

"Nothing and everything was wrong," I said at last. "I've always felt it." A sharp movement of Kitty's body confirmed my deep, old suspicion that she hated me.

He went back further than I expected.

"His relations with his father and mother, now?"

"His father was old when he was born, and always was a little jealous of him. His mother was not his sort. She wanted a stupid son who would have been satisfied with shooting."

He laid down a remark very softly, like a hunter setting a snare.

"He turned, then, to sex with a peculiar need."

It was Margaret who spoke, shuffling her feet awkwardly under her chair.

"Yes, he was always dependent."

We gaped at her who said this of our splendid Chris, and I saw that she was not as she had been. There was a directness of speech, a straight stare, that was for her a frenzy. "Doctor," she said, her mild voice roughened, "what's the use of talking? You can't cure him,"—she caught her lower lip with her teeth and fought back from the brink of tears,—"make him happy, I mean. All you can do is to make him ordinary."

"I grant you that's all I do," he said. It queerly seemed as though he was experiencing the relief one feels on meeting an intellectual equal. "It's my profession to bring people from various outlying districts of the mind to the normal. There seems to be a general feeling it's the place where they ought to be. Sometimes I don't see the urgency myself."

She continued without joy:

"I know how you could bring him back—a memory so strong that it would recall everything else in spite of his discontent."

The little man had lost in a moment his glib assurance, his knowingness about the pathways of the soul.

"Well, I'm willing to learn."

"Remind him of the boy," said Margaret.

The doctor ceased suddenly to balance on the balls of his feet.

"What boy?"

"They had a boy."

He looked at Kitty.

"You told me nothing of this!"

"I didn't think it mattered," she answered, and shivered

and looked cold, as she always did at the memory of her unique contact with death. "He died five years ago."

He dropped his head back, stared at the cornice, and said with the soft malignity of a clever person dealing with the slow-witted.

"These subtle discontents are often the most difficult to deal with." Sharply he turned to Margaret. "How would you remind him?"

"Take him something the boy wore, some toy he played with."

Their eyes met wisely.

"It would have to be you that did it."

Her face assented.

Kitty said:

"I don't understand. How does it matter so much?" She repeated it twice before she broke the silence that Margaret's wisdom had brought down on us. Then Dr. Anderson, rattling the keys in his trousers-pockets and swelling red and perturbed, answered:

"I don't know, but it does."

Kitty's voice soared in satisfaction.

"Oh, then it's very simple. Mrs. Grey can do it now. Jenny, take Mrs. Grey up to the nursery. There are lots of things up there."

Margaret made no movement, but continued to sit with her heavy boots resting on the edge of their soles. Dr. Anderson searched Kitty's face, exclaimed, "Oh, well!" and flung himself into an arm-chair so suddenly that the springs spoke. Margaret smiled at that and turned to me, "Yes, take me to the nursery, please." Yet as I walked beside her up the stairs I knew this compliance was not the indication of any melting of this new steely sternness. The very breathing that I heard as I knelt beside her at the nursery door and eased the disused lock seemed to come from a different and a harsher body than had been hers before. I did not wonder that she was feeling bleak, since in a few moments she was to go out and say the words that would end all her happiness, that would destroy all the gifts her generosity had so difficultly amassed. Well, that is the kind of thing one has to do in this life.

But hardly had the door opened and disclosed the empty, sunny spaces swimming with motes before her old sweetness flowered again. She moved forward slowly, tremulous and responsive and pleased, as though the room's loveliness was a gift to her. She stretched out her hands to the clear sapphire walls and the bright fresco of birds and animals with a young delight. So, I thought, might a bride go about the house her husband secretly prepared for her. Yet when she reached the hearth and stood with her hands behind her on the fireguard, looking about her at all the exquisite devices of our nursery to rivet health and amusement on our reluctant little visitor, it was so apparent that she was a mother that I could not imagine how it was that I had not always known it. It has sometimes happened that painters who have kept close enough to earth to see a heavenly vision have made pictures of the assumption of the Blessed Virgin which do indeed show women who could bring God into the world by the passion of their motherhood. "Let there be life," their suspended bodies seem to cry out to the universe about them, and the very clouds under their feet change into cherubim. As Margaret stood there, her hands pressed palm to palm beneath her chin and a blind smile on her face, she looked even so.

"Oh, the fine room!" she cried. "But where's his little cot?"

"It isn't here. This is the day nursery. The night nursery we didn't keep. It is just bedroom now."

Her eyes shone at the thought of the cockered childhood this had been.

"I couldn't afford to have two nurseries. It makes all the difference to the wee things." She hung above me for a little as I opened the ottoman and rummaged among Oliver's clothes. "Ah, the lovely little frocks! Did she make them? Ah, well, she'd hardly have the time, with this great house to see to. But I don't care much for baby frocks. The babies themselves are none the happier for them. It's all show." She went over to the rocking-horse and gave a ghostly child a ride. For long she hummed a tuneless song into the sunshine and retreated far away into some maternal dream. "He was too young for this," she said. "His daddy must have given him it. I knew it. Men always give them presents above their age, they're in such a hurry for them to grow up. We like them to take their time, the loves. But where's his engine? Didn't he love puffer-trains? Of course he never saw them. You're so far from the railway station. What a pity! He'd have loved them so. Dick was so happy when I stopped his pram on the railway-bridge on my way back from the shops, and he could sit up and see the puffers going by." Her distress that Oliver had missed this humble pleasure darkened her for a minute. "Why did he die! You didn't overtax his brain? He wasn't taught his letters too soon?"

"Oh, no," I said. I couldn't find the clothes I wanted. "The only thing that taxed his little brain was the prayers his Scotch nurse taught him, and he didn't bother much over them. He would say, 'Jesus, tender leopard,' instead of 'Jesus, tender shepherd,' as if he liked it better."

"Did you ever! The things they say! He'd a Scotch nurse.

They say they're very good. I've read in the papers the Queen of Spain has one." She had gone back to the hearth again, and was playing with the toys on the mantelpiece. It was odd that she showed no interest in my search for the most memorable garment. A vivacity which played above her tear-wet strength, like a ball of St. Elmo's fire on the mast of a stout ship, made me realize she still was strange. "The toys he had! His nurse didn't let him have them all at once. She held him up and said, 'Baby, you must choose!' and he said, 'Teddy, please, Nanny,' and wagged his head at every word."

I had laid my hand on them at last. I wished, in the strangest way, that I had not. Yet of course it had to be.

"That's just what he did do," I said.

As she felt the fine kid-skin of the clockwork dog, her face began to twitch.

"I thought perhaps my baby had left me because I had so little to give him. But if a baby could leave all this!" She cried flatly, as though constant repetition in the night had made it as instinctive a reaction to suffering as a moan, "I want a child! I want a child!" Her arms invoked the wasted life that had been squandered in this room. "It's all gone so wrong," she fretted, and her voice dropped to a solemn whisper. "They each had only half a life."

I had to steady her. She could not go to Chris and shock him not only by her news, but also by her agony. I rose and took her the things I had found in the ottoman and the toy cupboard.

"I think these are the best things to take. This is one of the blue jerseys he used to wear. This is the red ball he and his father used to play with on the lawn."

Her hard hunger for the child that was not melted into a tenderness for the child that had been. She looked brood-

89

ingly at what I carried, then laid a kind hand on my arm.

"You've chosen the very things he will remember. Oh, you poor girl!"

I found that from her I could accept even pity.

She nursed the jersey and the ball, changed them from arm to arm, and held them to her face.

"I think I know the kind of boy he was—a man from the first." She kissed them, folded up the jersey, and neatly set the ball upon it on the ottoman, and regarded them with tears. "There, put them back. That's all I wanted them for. All I came up here for."

I stared.

"To get Chris's boy," she moaned. "You thought I meant to take them out to Chris?" She wrung her hands; her weak voice quavered at the sternness of her resolution. "How can I?"

I grasped her hands.

"Why should you bring him back?" I said. I might have known there was deliverance in her yet.

Her slow mind gathered speed.

"Either I never should have come," she pleaded, "or you should let him be." She was arguing not with me, but with the whole hostile, reasonable world. "Mind you, I wasn't sure if I ought to come the second time, seeing we both were married and that. I prayed and read the Bible, but I couldn't get any help. You don't notice how little there is in the Bible really till you go to it for help. But I've lived a hard life and I've always done my best for William, and I know nothing in the world matters so much as happiness. If anybody's happy, you ought to let them be. So I came again. Let him be. If you knew how happy he was just pottering round the garden. Men do love a garden. He could just go on. It can go on so easily." But there was a shade of doubt in her voice; she was pleading not only with me, but with fate. "You wouldn't let them take him away to the asylum. You wouldn't stop me coming. The other one might, but you'd see she didn't. Oh, do just let him be!

"Put it like this." She made such explanatory gestures as I have seen cabmen make over their saucers of tea round a shelter. "If my boy had been a cripple,—he wasn't; he had the loveliest limbs,—and the doctors had said to me, 'We'll straighten your boy's legs for you, but he will be in pain all the rest of his life,' I'd not have let them touch him.

"I seemed to have to tell them that I knew a way. I suppose it would have been sly to sit there and not tell them. I told them, anyhow. But, oh, I can't do it! Go out and put an end to the poor love's happiness. After the time he's had, the war and all. And then he'll have to go back there! I can't! I can't!"

I felt an ecstatic sense of ease. Everything was going to be right. Chris was to live in the interminable enjoyment of his youth and love. There was to be a finality about his happiness which usually belongs only to loss and calamity; he was to be as happy as a ring cast into the sea is lost, as a man whose coffin has lain for centuries beneath the sod is dead. Yet Margaret continued to say, and irritated me by the implication that the matter was not settled:

"I oughtn't to do it, ought I?"

"Of course not! Of course not!" I cried heartily, but the attention died in her eyes. She stared over my shoulder at the open door, where Kitty stood.

The poise of her head had lost its pride, the shadows under her eyes were black like the marks of blows, and all her loveliness was diverted to the expression of grief. She held in her arms her Chinese sleeve dog, a once-prized pet that had fallen from favor and was now only to be met whining upward for a little love at every passer in the corridors, and it sprawled leaf-brown across her white frock, wriggling for joy at the unaccustomed embrace. That she should at last have stooped to lift the lonely little dog was a sign of her deep unhappiness. Why she had come up I do not know, nor why her face puckered with tears as she looked in on us. It was not that she had the slightest intimation of our decision, for she could not have conceived that we could follow any course but that which was obviously to her advantage. It was simply that she hated to see this strange, ugly woman moving about among her things. She swallowed her tears and passed on, to drift, like a dog, about the corridors.

Now, why did Kitty, who was the falsest thing on earth, who was in tune with every kind of falsity, by merely suffering somehow remind us of reality? Why did her tears reveal to me what I had learned long ago, but had forgotten in my frenzied love, that there is a draft that we must drink or not be fully human? I knew that one must know the truth. I knew quite well that when one is adult one must raise to one's lips the wine of the truth, heedless that it is not sweet like milk, but draws the mouth with its strength, and celebrate communion with reality, or else walk forever queer and small like a dwarf. Thirst for this sacrament had made Chris strike away the cup of lies about life that Kitty's white hands held to him and turn to Margaret with this vast trustful gesture of his loss of memory. And helped by me, she had forgotten that it is the first concern of love to safeguard the dignity of the beloved, so that neither God in his skies nor the boy peering through the hedge should find in all time one possibility for contempt, and had handed him the trivial toy of happiness. We had been utterly negligent of his future, blasphemously careless of the divine essential of his soul. For if we left him in his magic circle there would come a time when his delusion turned to a senile idiocy; when his joy at the sight of Margaret disgusted the flesh because his smiling mouth was slack with age; when one's eyes no longer followed him caressingly as he went down to look for the first primroses in the wood, but flitted here and there defensively to see that nobody was noticing the doddering old man. Gamekeepers would chat kindly with him, and tap their foreheads as they passed through the copse; callers would be tactful and dangle bright talk before him. He who was as a flag flying from our tower would become a queer-shaped patch of eccentricity on the country-side, the full-mannered music of his being would become a witless piping in the bushes. He would not be quite a man.

I did not know how I could pierce Margaret's simplicity with this last cruel subtlety, and turned to her, stammering. But she said:

"Give me the jersey and the ball."

The rebellion had gone from her eyes, and they were again the seat of all gentle wisdom.

"The truth's the truth," she said, "and he must know it."

I looked up at her, gasping, yet not truly amazed; for I had always known she could not leave her throne of righteousness for long, and she repeated, "The truth's the truth," smiling sadly at the strange order of this earth.

We kissed not as women, but as lovers do; I think we each embraced that part of Chris the other had absorbed by her love. She took the jersey and the ball, and clasped them as though they were a child. When she got to the door she stopped and leaned against the lintel. Her head fell back; her eyes closed; her mouth was contorted as though she swallowed bitter drink.

I lay face downward on the ottoman and presently heard her poor boots go creaking down the corridors. Through the feeling of doom that filled the room as tangibly as a scent I stretched out to the thought of Chris. In the deep daze of devotion which followed recollection of the fair down on his cheek, the skin burned brown to the rim of his gray eyes, the harsh and diffident masculinity of him, I found comfort in remembering that there was a physical gallantry about him which would still, even when the worst had happened, leap sometimes to the joy of life. Always, to the very end, when the sun shone on his face or his horse took his fences well, he would screw up his eyes and smile that little stiff-lipped smile. I nursed a feeble glow at that. "We must ride a lot," I planned. And then Kitty's heels tapped on the polished floor, and her skirts swished as she sat down in the arm-chair, and I was distressed by the sense, more tiresome than a flickering light, of some one fretting.

She said:

"I wish she would hurry up. She's got to do it sooner or later."

My spirit was asleep in horror. Out there Margaret was breaking his heart and hers, using words like a hammer, looking wise, doing it so well.

"Aren't they coming back?" asked Kitty. "I wish you'd look."

There was nothing in the garden; only a column of birds swinging across the lake of green light that lay before the sunset.

A long time after Kitty spoke once more:

"Jenny, do look again."

There had fallen a twilight which was a wistfulness of the earth. Under the cedar-boughs I dimly saw a figure

mothering something in her arms. Almost had she dissolved into the shadows; in another moment the night
would have her. With his back turned on this fading unhappiness Chris walked across the lawn. He was looking
up under his brows at the over-arching house as though it
were a hated place to which, against all his hopes, business
had forced him to return. He stepped aside to avoid a patch
of brightness cast by a lighted window on the grass; lights
in our house were worse than darkness, affection worse
than hate elsewhere. He wore a dreadful, decent smile; I
knew how his voice would resolutely lift in greeting us. He
walked not loose-limbed like a boy, as he had done that
very afternoon, but with the soldier's hard tread upon the
heel. It recalled to me that, bad as we were, we were yet not
the worst circumstance of his return. When we had lifted
the yoke of our embraces from his shoulders he would
go back to that flooded trench in Flanders, under that sky
more full of flying death than clouds, to that No-Man's-
Land where bullets fall like rain on the rotting faces of the
dead.

"Jenny, aren't they there?" Kitty asked again.

"They're both there."

"Is he coming back?"

"He's coming back."

"Jenny! Jenny! How does he look?"

"Oh,"—how could I say it?—"every inch a soldier."

She crept behind me to the window, peered over my
shoulder and saw.

I heard her suck in her breath with satisfaction.

"He's cured!" she whispered slowly. "He's cured!"

THE END

95

Made in the USA
Coppell, TX
18 January 2023

11256891R00059